D0960616

"**As the world's fastest reader (Guinness Book certified) I've read just about every business and marketing book in existence.** *The Irresistible Offer* by Mark Joyner is, by far, the clearest path to business success I've seen. If you want to make a business profitable (any business, small or large), *The Irresistible Offer* should be your starting point."

—Howard Berg, "The World's Fastest
Reader," Author of *Maximum Speed
Reading*, www.mrreader.com

"A three-second sale? Absolutely! Mark Joyner shows you how to easily construct an irresistible offer that will catapult you to success. You'll learn the secrets of how to take the spot in your customers' mind that your business deserves. **Don't let your competitors get this information before you do.**"

—Kenrick Cleveland, Author of *Maximum
Persuasion*, www.maxpersuasion.com

"Mark Joyner is not only one of the smartest and most successful Internet marketers, but also someone who truly understands the value of honesty and integrity. *The Irresistible Offer* will open your eyes about a crucial, but often-overlooked, area of copywriting. **His rule for how to find the right free bonuses—something you won't see elsewhere—is worth the price of the book right there.**"

—Shel Horowitz, Award-winning Author of
*Principled Profit: Marketing That Puts
People First* and Founder of the
international Business Ethics Pledge,
www.principledprofits.com

"Get the offer right, and everything else becomes easy. **In the right hands, this book is a prescription for millions.**"

—Paul Myers, Editor, *TalkBiz News*,
talkbiznews.com

"**If I had to choose one modern marketing genius to learn from, it would be Mark Joyner.** *The Irresistible Offer* belongs in the hands of everyone wanting to wildly succeed in business."

—Randy Gilbert, a.k.a. "Dr. Proactive," Host
of *The Inside Success Show*,
TheInsideSuccessShow.com

"*The Irresistible Offer* is an incredible book. There are a lot of theoretical books on marketing. Not this one. Mark Joyner delivers proven strategies based on actual results gleaned from millions of dollars in real-world testing. **Anyone who follows the formulas presented is sure to quickly see incredible results.**"

—Shawn Casey, Author of *Mining Gold on
the Internet*, www.ShawnCasey.com

"Mark Joyner recognized **the missing link in many marketing books** by focusing on one of the most compelling reasons a prospect will buy—the use of an irresistible offer. The Irresistible Offer is the driving force that propels a prospect to make the big decision to buy your product or service. Up until now there hasn't been a book that has focused entirely on this important but often-overlooked subject. Mark Joyner captures all of the psychology, science, and art of creating The Irresistible Offer and presents it in a very easy to understand manner. **I urge you to read it.**"

—Joe Sugarman, Chairman, BluBlocker
Corporation, blublocker.com

"**I'm going to rave about this masterpiece to everyone I know.** Even if you aren't in business you can apply this to every part of your life. It's inspiring in every aspect and I urge you to read it! I guarantee it will change your life."

—Sam Heyer, President of Magga Marketing, Inc., maggamarketing.com

"Mark Joyner plunges to the heart of marketing—crafting the offer you can't refuse—and reveals **secret after proven secret guaranteed to pump fresh power into your sales process**. Anyone seriously bent on transforming their revenue stream into a wild cascade owes it to themselves to absorb and implement Mark's advice."

—John Du Cane, CEO, Dragon Door Publications, www.dragondoor.com

"In *The Irresistible Offer*, not only does Mark Joyner give **step-by-step instructions** on how to create powerful offers that allow you to outshine your competitors, but the real gemstone is that he tells you how to craft mind-blowing offers never before seen that **scare the competition completely out of the race**. If you're someone who thinks you could never sell anything to anyone, as I once did, the only way you can fail after reading this brilliant but down-to-earth marketing cornucopia is if you do absolutely nothing."

—Donna Knight, Consultant, Founder of EbookQueen.com

"This amazing little book **ought to be required reading for any advertising executive, politician, marketer, or even member of the clergy** before they engage in any type of promotional campaign. What a wonderfully refreshing perspective!"

—Dr. Bill Nieporte, Pastor, Entrepreneur, ezinesuccess.com

"I've read every book on marketing printed in the last 150 years. This is the first breakthrough in over 50 years. A truly brilliant, practical, and inspiring book. Destined to be a classic and a collectible. It's a masterpiece."

—Joe Vitale, Author of *The Attractor Factor*, mrfire.com

The Irresistible Offer is a remarkable book that will transform your business and personal life. Mark Joyner's Great Formula is the **simplest and most powerful method of achieving success I've come across**. If you follow the suggestions in *The Irresistible Offer* you will develop an endless stream of happy customers, eager to buy from you again and again. Mark Joyner's new book is a textbook on how business should be done."

—Richard Webster, Author of more than 80 books, including *Seven Secrets to Success*, psychic.co.nz

"Mark Joyner is pure genius and incredibly crazy: he's giving away the secrets that make marketers millions and millions of dollars. *The Irresistible Offer* is incredibly detailed and **surprisingly very easy to read**. Mark explains **in simple language** what you won't find in other marketing books—how to create wealth by getting inside the mind of your customers and make your products absolutely irresistible. **I couldn't put the darn thing down.**"

—Tom Wood, CEO/President, Mastery Media, Inc., masterytv.com

"Clearly written, insightful and intelligent, *The Irresistible Offer* is **a *must read* for marketing novices and pros alike**. Mark Joyner shows that his true genius lies in being able to take a complex subject and distill it down to its essence in a concise and understandable fashion. I highly recommend this book to anyone who is interested in selling online or offline."

—Mel Strocen, CEO, Jayde Online Network, exactseek.com

"Genius. Joyner leans over your shoulder and delivers **the missing piece to the marketing puzzle**. Only a master can deliver information so clearly that the mind has no choice but to focus obsessively and devour every word. This book truly delivers the key to the entire process, and gives you examples from industry giants who used these skills you now hold in your hands to make massive fortunes. We couldn't put it down. One power-packed punch after the next had us spellbound and **gave us 'aha' moments almost every time we turned the page**."

—Skye & Jason Mangrum, Creators, "The World's First Manifestation Software," usemanifestsoftware.com

"Mark Joyner's book is absolutely on the mark and brilliant. It's packed with bite-sized chunks of practical wisdom, **breakthrough insights**, and unique sales and marketing tips. This book will become very dog-eared and worn, so you may want to get two!"

—Jim Fleck, Author of *Millionaire Kids, Millionaire Parents*

"The pages flow from start to finish with scientifically sound principles and marketing strategy. **Every page bursts with immediately practical guidelines** and strategy for applying the elusive obvious that nearly everyone seems to overlook outright in marketing their products and services.

"This is the stuff genius is made of, thinking in new directions and bringing new light to profitably grow your business. Mark Joyner offers an entertaining and balanced blend of marketing psychology and buyer behavior. I found myself rereading chapters and fiercely taking notes on how I'll leverage his ideas.

"**The reach of this contagious book far exceeds modern marketing. It overflows in applications relevant to salespeople, managers, schoolteachers, and parents, to name a few.**

"I firmly believe Mark Joyner is one of the great marketers of our generation. This book is a fascinating, intriguing presentation of forward-looking findings and insights spurring new awareness, causing you to completely rethink your company's marketing strategy. A real eye-opener describing in detail what we all urgently need and unmistakably overlook, The Irresistible Offer.

—Joe Soto, NLP Trainer,
persuasiontraining.com

"This should be canonized as marketing scripture. The Irresistible Offer now has a place on my shelf among the marketing classics."

—Russell Brunson, Author of
www.ConquerYourNiche.com

THE **IRRESISTIBLE** OFFER

How to Sell Your Product or Service in 3 Seconds or Less

Mark Joyner

WILEY

John Wiley & Sons, Inc.

Published by John Wiley & Sons, Inc., Hoboken, New Jersey.
Published simultaneously in Canada.

For general information on our other products and services please contact our
Customer Care Department within the United States at (800) 762-2974, outside
the United States at (317) 572-3993 or fax (317) 572-4002.

Wiley also publishes its books in a variety of electronic formats. Some content that
appears in print may not be available in electronic books. For more information
about Wiley products, visit our web site at www.Wiley.com.

Library of Congress Cataloging-in-Publication Data:

Joyner, Mark, 1968-
    The irresistible offer : how to sell your product or service in 3 seconds or
less / Mark Joyner.
        p.   cm.
    ISBN-13 978-0-471-73894-7 (cloth)
    ISBN-10 0-471-73894-8 (cloth)
  1. Marketing.   2. Selling.   I. Title.
    HF5415.J68   2005
    658.85—dc22   2005006844

10 9 8 7 6 5 4 3 2

CONTENTS

Preface   xi

Acknowledgments   xv

About the Author   xix

INTRODUCTION   (Three Seconds)   1

CHAPTER 1   The Magic Window   3

CHAPTER 2   The Core Imperative of Business   5

CHAPTER 3   The Big Four Questions   9

CHAPTER 4   What Is The Irresistible Offer?   15

CHAPTER 5   What Is *Not* The Irresistible Offer?   25

CHAPTER 6   Elements of The Irresistible Offer   35

CHAPTER 7   The Great Formula   55

CHAPTER 8   Offer Intensifiers   77

CHAPTER 9   The Offer Continuum   99

CONTENTS

CHAPTER 10 Great Offers through History   113

CHAPTER 11 Word of Mouth from Flaming Lips   125

APPENDIX A Selling Yourself in Three Seconds
                or Less   183

APPENDIX B A Note to Salesmen   207

Glossary   211

Index   215

 **PREFACE**

One could present a compelling case that marketing is destroying this planet.

Over time, marketers have discovered that the easiest way to sell something is to appeal to our basest needs and to exploit the weaknesses inherent in our psychology. For example, rather than walk our prospects through a logical buying decision and help them to purchase something that will genuinely help them, we con them into thinking that our Widgets will give them happiness and unlimited access to attractive members of the opposite sex. This is but one of the many tricks up the marketer's sleeve employed in conning the average consumer into making illogical buying decisions.

The average American goes deep into debt buying silly (and sometimes downright harmful) things that he simply does not need. This process has not just pushed the average consumer into debt; it has lowered his values as well.

When you are bombarded with messages day after day that present a world where selfishness, shallowness, and greed are the ultimate ideals, it's hard not to start believing that world is your own as well.

PREFACE

This book presents an alternative to the marketing of the past. I believe that a business can be immensely profitable and still operate with a high degree of integrity. I write this book not only with the intention of sparing the public further mental torture performed by the marketing community, but also to help business avoid its own demise.

I predict that as the debt rate rises and consumers better educate themselves through the unprecedented access to information given by the Internet, tolerance for the marketing methods of the past will drop considerably.

An angry and educated consumer is a dangerous foe for the marketer to face.

Soon, businesses will be scrambling for alternatives.

This book presents not just an alternative, but *the* alternative. This method of marketing has been proven time and again, but it has never been named. Using this method, you can literally close a deal in the mind of your prospect within the first three seconds of coming into contact with your marketing.

I've named this method "The Irresistible Offer," and the following pages deconstruct it and dissect it so that you can immediately apply it to your business for dramatic effect. This book is your essential survival guide for the emerging business battlefield of the twenty-first century. Ignore these lessons at your own peril.

Individuals and salespeople can benefit greatly from these pages as well.

In the Appendix "Selling Yourself in Three Seconds or Less," I explain how you can apply this technology to literally every aspect of your life. I then show salespeople how they can use this information to sell within a good ethical framework and still boost their sales to a level far beyond what they are experiencing now.

 # ACKNOWLEDGMENTS

When an author lists only his name on the cover of his work, it is really an exercise in ego and ungratefulness.

Without the help of a great many people, this book would not at all be possible.

First, there are countless books on the topics of business and marketing that have inspired me and provided clues to the discovery of this method.

Although a great deal of this book takes a hostile stance toward the marketing of the past, it's done with a great deal of respect, love, and admiration. I, too, was among the pre-TIO (The Irresistible Offer) era, which this book attempts to bring to an abrupt end. The brunt of that hostility could rightfully be directed at the Mark Joyner of yesterday as well. I hope that my peers in this field will agree that marketing has, indeed, gone too far and that this book may serve as a rallying cry for a new order.

With that said, I couldn't possibly list all of the authors, business owners, and marketing professionals who have inspired me here. Allow me to narrow them down to the list I may call "friends" and narrow that list down even further to those who have been closest to, or had the greatest impact on, me during the writing of this book.

So, allow me to thank my friends, in business and in the real world.

First, to the old-school direct marketers who have blessed me with their wisdom: Ted Nicholas, who has always inspired me with his integrity, his knowledge, and his spirit. Gary Bencivenga, with whom I have only recently come into contact and who, in that brief time, has managed to blow my mind. Gary Halbert, one of the cleverest (and most closely shaven) men on the planet, with whom I've shared many a meal and many a secret in the cafes of South Beach.

Next, to that dangerous pack of Internet marketers on the prowl: Matt Gill and Kevin Wilke, good friends and brothers always. Joe Vitale, whom I would invite in to my foxhole to go to battle, any day of the week and twice on Sundays—you are a true friend. Mike Merz, quite possibly the nicest guy I've never met face to face. Paul Myers, who may in fact be the last piece of sanity holding this crazy world together—thank you for your tireless fights for the truth. Chayden Bates, who is hiding out, but quietly plotting to take over the world and may very well succeed. Tom Antion, Tom Wood, Mike Filsaime, Russell Brunson, Josh Anderson, Shawn Casey, Brett Rademacher, Kimberly Gordon, Craig Perrine, Rob Fighter, Michel Fortin, Jim Fleck, Ankesh Kothari, Nick Temple, Frank Mullen, and Corey Rodl may he rest in peace.

Acknowledgments

Next to some various friends in business . . . Otto von Schulze, the president of the American Conservatory of Music, thanks for your friendship and for sharing your vision for the future. Mary Mazullo, thanks for your unending kindness and for being such a shining example. The good folks at Waymaker—may your noble vision soon become a reality. Richard Webster who has proven himself to be a great friend and a stalwart defender of all loud-mouthed self-promoters everywhere. The New Zealand Society of Authors, every one of whom I hope will some day have #1 best-sellers "the real way" or otherwise. To my dance teacher Claudia, you have made me a better person.

All of the old Aesop crew, most notably Virginia, Tom, Kevin, Tannaz, Tony, and Rooein (the ones who were there all the way to the end).

My real-world friends and family (many of the above should be in this list, but I'm a sucker for organization): Jim and the two Sarahs, Brande, Brook, Morgan, Bowen, Dad, Mom (may she rest in peace), Sam and Belinda, Carolyn and Vernon, Lisa; John; Erica and Kylie, Joe, Beth, Mike, Brad, Nichole, Harry; Graciella and Christian, Kerensa and Phil, Mark; Christine; Anna; and Lindsey, Jim and Elizabeth, Mr. and Mrs. Dimo, Sun and John, Sue Hyun, and many others.

To the people who have helped make this book possible on a very practical level: the staff at Wiley, Matt, Tamara, Shannon, Michelle, and others. Thank you for your incredible patience, support, and encouragement. You are the true professionals. To the incomparable Bill Plympton for blessing me with the superb cover art for this book.

ACKNOWLEDGMENTS

A special thanks to the priests of the Blessed Sacrament Catholic Church in Los Angeles who inspired me in my darkest days.

My bookkeeper Lili. You and your family have always been by my side during the greatest triumphs and the seemingly insurmountable challenges. You have inspired me and supported me in immeasurable ways and for that I'll always be grateful.

My P.A. Anna. You have added organization to my otherwise chaotic life and have helped me in ways I never appropriately express. Thanks for your never-ending confidence in me, your moral support, and your smile. I hope to always count you and Mark among my family.

Finally, my fiancée S. You're still my angel after all these years.

ABOUT THE AUTHOR

Mark Joyner is the former CEO of Aesop Marketing Corporation, #1 best-selling author of *MindControl Marketing.com*, and one of the early e-commerce pioneers.

A former U.S. Army officer and a cold war veteran of Military Intelligence, he turned his then one-man operation (Aesop) into a multimillion dollar corporation with customers in every Internet-connected country on the globe.

Mark pioneered many of the technologies now in common use on the Internet (such as remotely hosted ad tracking and the remotely locked client-side ASP model), is widely recognized as being responsible for popularizing the use of electronic books (e-books), launched many web sites that reached the Top 100 list of the most visited web sites in the world, and wrote an electronic book in 1994, which was downloaded over 1,000,000 times.

After closing Aesop's doors Mark has focused on writing and doing private consulting work. His clients quite happily pay him $2,000 per hour for his private business consultations.

Mark has a Bachelor of Science in Psychology, was trained in the Korean language at the Defense Language

ABOUT THE AUTHOR

Institute, has served both the U.S. and Republic of Korea governments while in the U.S. Army and has been awarded for his service by the U.S. Army, the Republic of Korea Army, The Korean Consulate General, the Defense Language Institute, and the President of the United States.

You can learn what Mark is working on by signing up for his free newsletter at www.MarkJoyner.name.

INTRODUCTION

(Three Seconds)

Tick.

Tick.

Tick.

There are 86,400 seconds in a day.

You have exactly 3 of them to capture the mind of your prospect.

People today are impatient, and rightfully so. They are bombarded with thousands of marketing messages a day. If they were to respond to every message they see, they would be utterly paralyzed.

Today, consumers are *forced* to make quick evaluations as a matter of survival.

With this in mind, those three seconds consumers give us are actually quite generous. In those three seconds sales are made, deals are closed, and empires are built. Do you know what to do in those three seconds?

Think for a moment before you answer. . . . If you're like 99.6 percent of the business world, you *don't* know what to do. You don't know at all.

Don't worry. The rest of this book will show you.

CHAPTER 1

The Magic Window

What if you had a magic window?

Whenever you look through that window, everything that is false disappears, and only the beautiful and true remain.

If you could look into the business world through such a window how long would it take you to match the riches of Bill Gates or Donald Trump?

All false theories and ideas would vanish.

No false moves could be made.

You could only think and do what is right and profitable and good.

It would be impossible to fail.

Once you understand the simple concept that is about to be revealed to you, you will have such a magic window on the business world.

That concept is *The Irresistible Offer.*

Once you get it, you'll be absolutely and utterly unstoppable.

Read on.

CHAPTER 2

The Core
Imperative
of Business

The focus of the following pages is nothing less than the *Core Imperative of Business.*

By extension, one may say it's even the core imperative of anything you do in your life, but business will serve as an apt metaphor for now.

I want to show you an extremely efficient form of marketing that cuts right to heart of your prospects' mind and will have them ready to buy your products, your services, and your ideas almost instantly.

This concept will give you a clear starting point that will let you see through a morass of business trends and theories.

So let's get to it. What is the Core Imperative of Business?

It's quite simple, really. Just think about it.

In order to do business in this world, what is the one thing you need? The one thing you absolutely, positively cannot do without?

It's not a business card.

It's not an office.

No, Mr. High-Tech, it's not your BlackBerry.

And you know what? It's not even a product.

The core of all business goes back to when human beings first began entering into the most rudimentary transactions with each other, when cavemen traded a wooly mammoth pelt in exchange for a new club.

From the dawn of time, all business can be boiled down to one single thing.

An offer.

That's right. An offer.

A *quid pro quo.*

This for that.

You scratch my back, I'll scratch yours.

What does the ice cream man offer? *You give me money. I give you refreshment.*

What does a banker offer? *You let me borrow your money, I'll give you some interest.*

What does your government offer? *You pay us taxes, and we'll protect you from the barbarian hoards.*

What do hospitals, haberdashers, and hookers all do?

They make offers.

Business simply does not get done—in fact, it doesn't even start—until an offer is made.

The Core Imperative of Business is simply this: Make an offer.

Some will say I'm oversimplifying. They will say I'm underestimating the value of public relations, of marketing smoke and mirrors, of surveys and focus groups. They will say, "You should sell the sizzle, not the steak."

Well, actually, there's a word for selling sizzle without steak. It's called a scam.

All of the sales finesse in the world won't make up for a remorseful, dissatisfied buyer if you don't address the buyer's core issues. Address these core issues, however, and you will not just have a sale, but a customer for life.

These core issues take the form of what I call the Big Four Questions.

CHAPTER 3

The Big
Four Questions

During the sales process, an *Unspoken Inner Dialogue* takes place.

No matter how much confidence we radiate to the world around us, fear, skepticism, and insecurities are playing games within our consciousness. Even within (perhaps *especially* within) the most blustery, cocky person you can imagine, this Unspoken Inner Dialogue is happening. Fears and insecurities are silently being voiced:

Do people hate me?

I can't believe I said that. Did that sound stupid?

Does he love me?

Do I look fat in these pants?

There is a very specific form of this dialogue that occurs whenever anyone is making a buying decision of any form. Don't minimize the importance of this Unspoken Inner Dialogue. If you don't address your buyer's comfort level, your job of selling becomes significantly more difficult.

And if you try to finesse your way around these fears with sizzle instead of steak, the consequences of making such a sale—consequences that will come back to haunt you later with a very unhappy buyer—are worse than making no sale at all.

So, understanding that this Unspoken Inner Dialogue is taking place, your offer must answer the *Big Four Questions*. The Big Four Questions are the Unspoken Inner Dialogue of your prospects when you try to sell to them.

Here are the first two:

Question 1: *What are you trying to sell me?*

Question 2: *How much?*

Let's look at these questions in tandem. Put them together, and your buyer is asking, "What is your offer?" Your communication must reassure that ongoing Unspoken Inner Dialogue that you are offering a commodity of acceptable quality for a reasonable price.

Give me five dollars, and I'll give you a glass of water.

Give me $5,000, and I'll remove your swollen appendix.

Give me $100, and I'll (deleted!) . . .

If, at the core of your sales process, your offer is not a good or a fair one, then only fools will buy. And, if you have fooled someone into buying your product, you won't have that customer for very long. In the long term, a business built on such a shaky foundation will not last.

You can always sucker someone into giving you money, but you can only do it once.

A master—one who knows how to make a quality offer—will wow the customer once, and wow him again and again and again until both buyer and seller have happily prospered. Such is the way millions and billions are made.

Once the offer has been made, there are still two questions that must always be addressed in the prospect's mind.

Question 3: *Why should I believe you?*

Indeed, why *should* someone believe you?

This question goes to the core of buyer insecurity. Sometimes, offers can sound fantastic on the surface, but therein lies the problem—they sound too good to be true.

People have to trust that they're not dealing with a charlatan peddling snake oil before they are willing to hand over their money. An offer only works if it has credibility behind it. Again, only a fool would hand over money for nothing, and you don't want a fool for a customer.

Question 4: *What's in it for me?*

Wait a minute . . . We just answered the question, "What are you trying to sell me?" Isn't this the same thing?

Not exactly. When people ask, "What's in it for me?" they are trying to figure out how they benefit. People buy products, but what they want are "benefits." You buy the Bentley, but what's really in it for you is the prestige that comes with owning one.

You buy the health food, but what's really in it for you is a better quality of life (and more of it).

Most marketers see this as the core question to be answered. Its importance is obvious—if there is nothing in it for me, why should I waste my time listening to you?

This question is so often pondered by marketers that we shorten it to "WIIFM." However, to focus on this question alone is folly. If you focus solely on WIIFM, your marketing will seem pitchy and solicitous.

The same marketers who tell you erroneously to "sell the sizzle and not the steak" will also say "sell your benefits not your features." This approach is, in fact, effective in the short term, but not in the long term.

Why?

There's a marketing axiom that's been around for a long time: "People make their decisions based on emotion and justify them with logic." There is some great truth to this phrase.

Apply that saying to the Four Questions. The first three questions address the buyer's logic, the last one goes to

If you had three seconds to sell yourself, what would you say?

What kind of a nightmare would it be if you were tongue-tied?

For more than one person, that terrible nightmare has actually happened.

Here is one famous example: In 1980, Ted Kennedy ran against President Jimmy Carter for the Democratic nomination for president. Senator Kennedy agreed to a one-hour interview on CBS to discuss his candidacy.

The interviewer began the hour by asking Senator Kennedy a simple question. "Why do you want to be president?" This was Ted Kennedy's chance to make an offer to the nation, to say, "You make me president, and I will make you safe, secure, and prosperous." Instead, he couldn't answer the question. He couldn't come up with the words. He was tongue-tied. He never made the offer. And you know the rest of the story. Ted Kennedy never became president, or even the Democratic nominee.

emotion. Address the emotional decision alone and, again, you'll only have fools for customers.

But, it won't be that way for you when your moment comes to make your offer.

You won't just make an offer. You'll make The Irresistible Offer.

What is The Irresistible Offer?

How is one made?

Could it be as simple and effective as it sounds?

Yes, it really is.

Not only that, but the benefits are more far-reaching than you may realize now. Further, the applications of this technology stretch way beyond the bounds of marketing and advertising. As you'll see, you can apply this to almost every aspect of your life to great effect.

CHAPTER 4

What Is The Irresistible Offer?

et's start with a definition. *The Irresistible Offer* is an *identity-building offer central to a product, service, or company* where the believable return on investment is communicated so clearly and efficiently that it's immediately apparent you'd have to be a fool to pass it up.

The full meaning of these words will not make an impression on you just yet. Don't worry. They will in a few moments.

The Irresistible Offer cuts through all the noise and clutter. It creates an itch that the buyer has to scratch. Such an offer makes doing business with you so easy and obviously beneficial that you stand out clearly from the crowd. People remember you. People can't move quickly enough to give you their money.

The Irresistible Offer sparks the customer's imagination and creates an urgent, gotta-have-it-now, buying frenzy.

Think for a few minutes, and maybe you can come up with a few examples of such an offer. I'll give you a great one in a moment.

Do you not own a product, service, or company?

Do you think The Irresistible Offer is not for you?

Think again.

The fact is, almost all of us are involved at some step of the sales process somewhere. Further, we must all sell ourselves (be it to customer, boss, kids, spouse, or a potential lover).

Business is the chosen metaphor for this book for two reasons. First, because it is the most common application of this technology. Second, because everyone can understand the frame of reference of business. We are all de facto experts in advertising, since we see so much of it every day.

If your aim in reading this book is learning how to sell yourself, everything will fall into place for you when we get to the chapter entitled "Selling Yourself in Three Seconds or Less." However, the foundation you're learning now is an essential first step.

So, read on. . . .

But you may be wondering, "If The Irresistible Offer is so powerful and dynamic, why aren't you reading about it in every other marketing book on the shelves?" Good question.

Every marketing book I've ever read has danced around this topic. It's been danced around, but it hasn't been named. That's not to knock my peers in this field. There is some great advice to be found out there and some highly effective theories on how to do business. Everything here is built on the shoulders of those great books.

But there's a problem with the marketing approaches of the past.

If you don't start with The Irresistible Offer as the core of your business approach, then all of the grand theories and marketing trickery of the world amount to nothing more than throwing a coat of glossy paint on a rickety wooden shack. It could be the world's greatest paint job, but there isn't much of a real estate market for well-painted shacks.

The Irresistible Offer, by contrast, allows you to create a castle. You can make a lot of business mistakes—or, to continue the metaphor, you can paint the castle a really crappy color or put tacky pink flamingos on the grounds in front of the drawbridge—but, you've still got a castle. You've still got a solid foundation.

17

THE ANTITHESIS OF OLD-SCHOOL MARKETING THROUGH COERCION

Here's another way of looking at it.

The Irresistible Offer, properly executed, is the antithesis to marketing through coercion. In a way, this book is the yin to my last book's (*MindControlMarketing.com*, Los Angeles: Steel Icarus, 2002) yang. That book was all about the many ways marketers cloud the minds of customers to get them to buy.

This book is about not having to do so.

With The Irresistible Offer, you don't need Mind Control Marketing (MCM). That is not to say that you can't use a little art or MCM to increase the effectiveness of your offer. The point is you wouldn't *need* any. The psychological power of The Irresistible Offer in itself is strong enough.

HOW THE IRRESISTIBLE OFFER REVOLUTIONIZED AN INDUSTRY

Let's talk about the way The Irresistible Offer revolutionized an entire industry. First, if you live in the United States, put this book down, go grab a phone book, and come back.

You're back? Got the phone book? Good. Now, look up "pizza" in the Yellow Pages.

No surprise there, right? If you're in a populated area of almost any size, you probably find at least a few pizza joints listed.

Now, I want you to comb through the rest of the phone book and tell me if you can find any other type of food that has its own category listing in the yellow pages.

Hold on. . . . Let me save you several days of searching. There aren't any.

If you own any other kind of food establishment—Chinese, burgers, barbecue, seafood, you name it—then you're listed under restaurants. You're in the restaurant business. If you own a pizza parlor, you're not in the restaurant business—you're in the pizza business.

Only one type of food has such a dominant role in the American culture that it has its own category in the phone book.

Pizza.

So, would it be possible for one man, one business to come out of nowhere and utterly dominate such a pervasive, nationwide, household-name type of industry?

And what if I told you he was up against several extremely well-established national brands? Most people would say "impossible" (especially if you understand the power of branding and positioning), but perhaps they don't know how Tom Monaghan used The Irresistible Offer.

Here's the story of a pizza chain that was relatively unknown for years until it launched a now legendary marketing campaign. Tom Monaghan started this business in

19

Ypsilanti, Michigan, in 1960 with the purchase of a single store called "Dominick's." When Tom chose to expand, the former owner of Dominick's wouldn't let him keep the name, so he had to come up with a new one. One of his employees suggested "Domino's" one night, and it stuck.

When Monaghan purchased the first store, he began with a 15-minute lesson in marketing from Dominick himself, and he was off and running. In 2004, there were 7,000 Domino's pizzerias, and they grossed $4,000,000,000 in sales annually.

What allowed him to build a $4 billion business from a single store?

> *The 30-minutes-or-free guarantee was as responsible for our growth as anything.*
> —Tom Monaghan

His rise to success wasn't overnight. Monaghan experienced some extreme ups and downs along the way (including a near bankruptcy and a royal suing by his franchise owners), but it wasn't until he developed the classic example of The Irresistible Offer (and one of history's greatest advertising campaigns) that Domino's began to explode.

Tom Monaghan knew people wanted the convenience of delivery pizza. They also liked their pizza piping hot. So he created the guarantee: "30 minutes or less . . . or it's free."

It's not an exaggeration to say that this took the pizza world by storm. By the time Domino's was forced to stop using the "30 minutes or it's free" campaign as the result of a lawsuit in 1993, they were the number-one pizza delivery company in the entire United States.

And the "30 minutes or it's free" guarantee became part of our lexicon.

We'd marvel at it (". . . no, but seriously, dude—how do they get it here so fast?! I bet they bake it in the vans!").

We'd joke about it (making "30 minutes or it's free" offers to young ladies, and such). Most importantly, though, we'd keep on buying it.

Now, here's what's amazing about the power of the way Domino's used The Irresistible Offer: Domino's Pizza sucked!

I know I'm not alone in that opinion. Domino's, back in the days when it was first taking the nation by storm, produced some truly awful pizza. We'd joke that you couldn't tell the difference between the pizza and the cardboard box. And we were only half-joking.*

---

*A disclaimer here: I *love* the Domino's of today. As I write this I'm living in the Domino's-less city of Auckland, New Zealand. We took a trip down to the capital city of Wellington a few months ago, and I was delighted to find a Domino's. Of course, my fiancée wasn't delighted that I cancelled our first-class dining reservations so that I could order pizza and Coke in our hotel room.

Yes, the pizza back then sucked, but it didn't matter. Domino's was backed by the seeds of The Irresistible Offer.

When people are hungry and don't want to go out, they would eat anything—even pizza that tastes like cardboard—as long as they could get it quickly.

And it says a great deal about how The Irresistible Offer can capture the attention of millions that, when Domino's finally had to end the 30-minute guarantee because of a multimillion lawsuit when one of its drivers ran over a pedestrian, it made international headlines.*

DECONSTRUCTING DOMINO'S

Let's analyze what made this offer work as well as it did.

If you're hungry, you don't have much time, and you need a hot meal, who you gonna call? The 30-minute pizza guys, of course. When other deliveries, perhaps tastier, are hit and miss, who are you going to rely on when you are hungry *right now?*

---

*Don't worry, you don't have to be engaged in a multimillion dollar high publicity lawsuit to benefit from The Irresistible Offer. There are other cases of pizza delivery drivers running over pedestrians, and it was only the Domino's fame that led that particular suit to be so famous. It's more of a testament to how effective their marketing was than it was to the danger of their drivers (who were no more so than others).

But the time wasn't the only selling point. It was 30 minutes or it was *free*. This tagline was the "Touchstone" that made the offer irresistible. (That's important, and we'll come back to it in a minute.)

It was almost like a challenge. People would make it a point to time the delivery guy to see if he was going to be late. It was a little like a lottery. You'd almost want them to be late in order to get a free pizza. Thus, The Irresistible Offer sparked more than just a marketing campaign. It became a cultural icon. And it made billions of dollars.

Now, there's a little more to it than you see now. One important point is that Domino's wouldn't have maintained their success if they had kept on tasting like cardboard (more on that shortly).

THE IRRESISTIBLE OFFER *MUST* BE YOUR STARTING POINT

What's important to know now is this: *The Irresistible Offer is so powerful that it* must *be the very core of your business. Before you engage in any other marketing activities, The Irresistible Offer must be your starting point.*

In the following chapters, I'll show you how to create The Irresistible Offer for your business. By the time you finish this book, you'll even be able to crank up the intense demand for your products or service to the point that your customers will be begging to do business with you.

Believe me, this can happen. I once used this system in an offer for a limited production item, and one of my customers who had already placed an order traveled 100 miles to our offices just to make sure in person his order made it through without a hitch. Soon, you'll know how you can get people that fired up too.

Read on.

CHAPTER **5**

What Is *Not* The Irresistible Offer?

hen it comes to sales hyperbole, words can have infinite meanings.

"New and Improved" might refer to a groundbreaking, innovative product. Then again, it might be the same old stuff with a new label slapped on the front and a little inconsequential tinkering with the ingredients.

"Biggest Sale Ever" might mean an unprecedented slashing of prices. Or, more likely than not, those are just words conjured up from a marketer's feverish imagination in a desperate attempt to drum up sales.

When it comes to The Irresistible Offer, though, I want to make it clear that there is no ambiguity. There is no room for interpretation. The Irresistible Offer is made up of specific, essential elements. We'll get to those in a few pages.

Before we get there, it might help to understand what The Irresistible Offer is *not.*

An Irresistible Offer Is *Not* a "Special Offer"

Special offers come and go. They're made for the moment, not for the long term. The Irresistible Offer, by contrast, is *central* to product, service, or company. It is the lifeblood. It simply can not be separated from your identity.

The Irresistible Offer (Upper Case) Is *Not* an "irresistible offer" (lower case)

An irresistible offer is an effective, but old marketing concept whereby one stacks on benefit after benefit and bonus after bonus until the buyer cries "enough!" and has to cave in to the pressure. An irresistible offer is not a new thing. The Irresistible Offer isn't either—it just hasn't been talked about before.

An Irresistible Offer Is *Not* a Statement of Fact

So, you've been in business for 20 years. No one cares, really. They might, but it's not an important enough fact to lead with in your marketing.

The Irresistible Offer Is *Not* a Statement of Bragging Rights

So, you're the biggest clothing store in Muskogee? Again, no one really cares, and even if they do, it's not enough on its own merits to get them to *buy now.*

The Irresistible Offer Is *Not* a Benefit

We're getting somewhere here, but we're still miles shy of Irresistible.

The Irresistible Offer Is *Not* a USP

Heck—no one can even agree on what it means! Let's take a look at a few of these more closely.

THE IRRESISTIBLE OFFER IS NOT A "SPECIAL OFFER"

First, let's make it clear that I'm not knocking Special Offers. Far from it. If you need a temporary boost in sales, a good special offer can be just the ticket. (Just don't overdo it. Too many too often will turn them into "not-so-special offers." Also, if you have specials every week [like many pizza parlors] customers may wait to do business with you until the next coupon arrives. They need to want you badly enough to jump over hurdles to get you.)

Here's the main difference. A Special Offer is a one-time deal. The Irresistible Offer is not. The Irresistible Offer is so central to the very heart of your business that it becomes your identity.

The power of this can be observed with another look at Domino's Pizza—now a decade after they ended their "30 minutes or its free" tagline. I ordered pizza from Domino's with some friends in 2003. The pizza came in about 45 minutes, and one of my friends looked at his watch and said, "Hey, isn't it supposed to be free?"

Back to Special Offers—again, they are still fantastic tools.

In fact, Special Offers and The Irresistible Offer can work together nicely. If you are going to make a Special Offer, you can use many of the same principles used to create The Irresistible Offer. In fact, Special Offers are much easier to create than The Irresistible Offer. Once you've created The Irresistible Offer for your product or business, you should be able to create a Special Offer with one arm tied behind your back and blindfolded.

Okay, let's took a look at each of these in more detail.

THE IRRESISTIBLE OFFER IS NOT A BENEFIT

Benefits can be remarkably powerful tools—unique benefits ever more so. As an offer, though, they only address one of the Big Four Questions—"what's in it for me?"

I've seen so many people make the critical mistake of using a benefit as the lead for their marketing pitches. It's tempting to do this, particularly if you have a very attractive and compelling benefit to display, but it's a huge error.

Leading with a benefit will capture your target's interest, but the interest is almost always tempered with skepticism— "What's the catch? Is this nice benefit meant to distract me from flaws elsewhere?" Then, you have to spend the rest of your marketing pitch addressing that cynicism and answering the remaining three of the Big Four Questions.

The Irresistible Offer addresses all of the Big Four in a highly efficient manner—leaving your consumer receptive, not skeptical, and in a frame of mind to buy, buy, buy.

THE IRRESISTIBLE OFFER IS NOT A USP

Unique Selling Proposition (USP) is a phrase that gets slung around quite freely in the marketing world. What is it, exactly? Well, that depends on who you talk to.

If you're talking to a direct marketing guru, they will emphasize that USP is synonymous with uniqueness. A USP, they will tell you, is what sets you apart from the competition in the marketplace. I attended a seminar once in which the speaker told us to make a list of all of our company's benefits and advantages, circle the ones that are unique, and that, he said, is your USP.

An interesting approach, but it might give you only a fraction of the power of The Irresistible Offer.

You get a different definition entirely from people who are involved in branding big-name products and companies. They will tell you that the USP is a statement of the core values of your brand.

One day, I had a long conversation with Steve Gursich, CEO of the legendary advertising agency GSD&M. This is the iconic agency that handles the accounts for Wal-Mart, American Airlines, and other megabusinesses.

We were discussing some ad copy I was writing as a favor for one of his companies, and the topic of USP came up. It became clear to me very quickly that we were operating under very different definitions of the term.

To clarify, I asked him, "What would you say is Wal-Mart's USP?" Without hesitation, he said, "Value, Loyalty, and Quality."

A direct marketer would tell you this is a terrible USP, but I don't know a single direct marketer who is responsible for the volume of sales that Wal-Mart is each year.

The approach obviously works like gangbusters for Wal-Mart, but their business, and the type of marketing they do, is unique. If you can create an infrastructure of thousands of stores and undercut all the competition on price because of your sheer buying power, perhaps this approach may work for you.

Further, this is but a small piece of the Wal-Mart picture, so it would be folly to model a tiny subset of their marketing mix without understanding how it fits into their big picture.

Let's try one more approach and see if it gets us close to what we're seeking.

Rosser Reeves is not a household name, but he was one of the greatest minds in the history of advertising. In his book *Reality in Advertising* (New York: Knopf, 1961) he said:

> Each advertisement must make a proposition to the consumer. Not just words, not just product puffery, not just show-window advertising. Each advertisement must say to each reader: "Buy this product and you will get this specific benefit."
>
> The proposition must be one that the competition either cannot, or does not, offer. It must be unique—either a uniqueness of the brand or a claim not otherwise made in that particular field of advertising.

It's a profound idea, isn't it? That gets us very close to our target, but we're still not quite there.

Like the direct marketers, Reeves seems to have believed that uniqueness per se was sufficient in itself. One of his great, classic campaigns reflected this concept. Remember the advertising for Anacin? "Anacin: The Pain Reliever Doctors Prescribe Most."

Those are seven very powerful words. Perhaps some of the best ad copy ever written. It makes you think, if doctors prescribe Anacin more than other pain relievers, then it must be pretty darned good at stopping headaches.

From a branding perspective, it's a great USP. When you're in the drug store deciding on a brand of aspirin to buy, you might very well be persuaded to buy the one that doctors prescribe most.

But it's not The Irresistible Offer.

Why not?

Because it merely makes you wonder about the best possible aspirin. It doesn't necessarily make you want to buy right now. The Irresistible Offer would not just be useful when you're in the store wondering which aspirin to buy—it would motivate you to drive out to the store and buy your brand.

Don't be lulled into the trap of thinking that uniqueness alone will make your sales revenues start climbing. Staying in the realm of drugstores, let's say that you market your shop as the only drugstore that offers live musical entertainment at the top of every hour. That might get some people interested in you as a novelty, but it won't necessarily translate into sales.

Again, uniqueness per se is not enough and is sometimes totally irrelevant.

Or what if you market the fact that you're the only drugstore in town with a pharmacist who speaks Japanese?

That's a unique benefit that will certainly pique the interest of the Japanese-speaking population, but that's just an Offer Intensifier (more on that later), not nearly as powerful as the Irresistible Offer itself.

It's not enough just to be unique.

By contrast, what if you market your pain reliever by saying, "Your headache is gone and you're feeling good in 10 minutes or your money back."

Is that a different approach? Will it have a different impact?

The Irresistible Offer requires several elements to make it truly irresistible.

And all you have to do to find out what they are is . . . go on to the next page.

CHAPTER 6

Elements of The Irresistible Offer

Okay, by this point, you're beginning to realize that The Irresistible Offer has the power to turn your business into a thriving, growing empire. No doubt, though, you have a few questions. Most, importantly . . .

How does one do it?

You are about to learn a few tools that will make creating The Irresistible Offer for your business a snap. Let's start with this—The Irresistible Offer is composed of three elements:

1. A *H*igh ROI Offer
2. A *T*ouchstone
3. *B*elievability

It's easy to remember these three core elements when you use the following handy mnemonic device. Think HTB—How to Be Rich? The Irresistible Offer, of course!

Let's take a closer look at each of these elements.

THE HIGH ROI OFFER

Remember the Core Imperative of Business—*make an offer!* Real business does not even begin until you do. It's called "quid pro quo." I give you this—you give me that. We both come away better for having made a deal.

It seems pretty fundamental, doesn't it? And yet so many businesses and entrepreneurs today are getting away from this basic principle. And the farther we stray from the Core Imperative, the more we confuse our customers and ultimately lose sales.

ROI means "Return on Investment." Every purchase is essentially an investment. And, if your customers are not getting something from you that is perceived as greater in value than what they are investing, then they're getting a negative return, and you're not going to be doing business very long.

Simply offer the customer a genuinely good deal, and your job of marketing suddenly becomes a hell of a lot easier.

Those businesses that have strayed from this Core Imperative often do so because their offers don't render a genuinely high ROI to the consumer. Businesses rationalize that ROI is all perception, so it becomes easy to justify the use of sales trickery to make the sale.

If the ROI is clear, no sales trickery is needed. You can get right down to business and spend more time making sales and less time weaving your loom of sales hypnosis.

Back in the 1950s and 1960s, movie theaters used to play this game all of the time. They would book cheap horror flicks and make the customers sign a waiver before entering the show, holding the theater owner blameless in case they should have a heart attack because of the movie's incredibly frightening scenes. The theaters had to use this gimmick because the movies were garbage. The return (entertainment value, or lack thereof) was not worth the customer's investment (ticket price and time spent in the theater), so the theater had to use cheesy tricks to draw attention away from the poor ROI.

You don't have to resort to these kinds of tricks to make your offer desirable. All you have to do is offer a truly high-value ROI. If you can't snap your fingers and turn your product into a great one, then add something that makes it great. Add some service, feature, or benefit—anything that will make your offer a truly great deal for the customer.

This is a good moment to return to the Domino's Pizza example from a few pages ago.

 *Warning:* Some businesses think they can improve their ROI by simply lowering their price. It makes sense that by lowering the cost you can improve the value for the customer, but that's a dangerous game. The economic graveyard is full of businesses who priced themselves out of existence by charging customers too little. You are in business, after all, to make a profit. There are ways to add value to your offer, and therefore to enhance customer appreciation, that do not detract from your own profit margins.

Domino's 30-minutes-or-it's-free offer was terrifically effective in capturing my attention, as well as that of a few million other customers. But if they didn't get their act together and make a better-tasting pizza, they wouldn't have lasted as long as they have. They had a great Touchstone (perhaps *the* quintessential touchstone), but they needed a higher ROI offer to continue thriving.

When I order Domino's today, I order it because it's fast, it's inexpensive, and it's delicious. In short, I'm getting a great return on my investment. If it weren't tasty, they may sucker me into buying another pizza or two if I were desperate, but I wouldn't go back for my Second Helping (more on that shortly).

Today, I'm not only a satisfied, loyal customer, but I'm spreading their marketing message for them, evangelizing to my friends about the quality of Domino's Pizza. (You can read further about how to make the most of this kind of Word of Mouth marketing, but the fact is that having a high ROI offer is 90 percent of the game. Word of Mouth without The Irresistible Offer is lukewarm at best. More on this shortly.)

You achieve the polar opposite result when you try to trick your customer. Trust me. I've been there too. I've been conned into making purchases that masqueraded as The Irresistible Offer, but in truth sorely lacked a core high ROI offer (or even a break-even point on my investment). In these cases, the businesses involved not only failed to win me over as a fan, they made a lifelong enemy out of me. There are cases when I've been sitting with friends, talking about bad companies who have done us wrong. Then, a new friend enters the circle, hears our stories, and passes them along to others. Thus, this poor-ROI company is being badmouthed by people who have never even been their customers—and the company deserves it.

What's worse, you only have to mess up once for this to happen. Even great companies screw up, and the buzz from that single mistake can have a huge impact. Winston Churchill said, "A lie will travel half-way around the globe before the truth even has a chance to put its pants on." Negative information has a way of spreading a lot faster than positive information, so it's doubly important that you not only satisfy but utterly delight your customers.

THE TOUCHSTONE

Never before in the history of modern man have we had so many marketing messages competing for our attention. TV ads, radio ads, direct mail, billboards, Internet banners, e-mail . . . you name it. Heck, I put down the tray table on an airplane a few weeks ago, and there was an ad in my face for a cell phone!

There is so much of it that most of it barely registers on our consciousness. Even some of the most creative approaches garner just a flicker of our attention and then get drowned out in a sea of marketing white noise.

What if you could cut through all of the static? What if you could capture your customer's attention, make yourself truly memorable, and put your customers in a frame of mind that makes them want to buy your product or service on the spot?

And what if all of this happened in less than three seconds?

The Touchstone of your Irresistible Offer can do just that. This is really where the sale takes place. After your touchstone, all you have to do is not screw up and the deal is done.

We're getting ahead of ourselves.

What's a touchstone? In short, it's a statement that addresses as many of the following points as possible:

✔ Here's what we are selling.
✔ Here's how much it will cost.

- ✔ Here's what's in for you.
- ✔ Here's why you should trust us.

If this sounds familiar from earlier in the book, it should. Remember the Big Four Questions?

And, *no matter what,* your Touchstone must say: *Here's a great offer. Here's a deal for you so great that you'd be a fool to pass it up.*

Now, before you run off and start constructing your Touchstone based upon what I just told you, you need to realize that simply communicating these different points is not, in itself, enough. It's not a grocery list. You must communicate these ideas in a particular way in order to have the desired effect on your customer.

The Stylistic Elements of a Great Touchstone

The following guidelines will provide some valuable clues.

Clarity

Don't make your customer try to interpret what you're saying. They won't bother. Go right to their minds with a crisp message that leaves nothing to the imagination.

Simplicity

People have enough complexity in their lives. They're not looking for more, particularly from someone trying to sell them something. Your Touchstone should be a simple statement that is easily understandable.

Brevity

Aren't you usually in a hurry? So is your customer. Respect that and keep it short. *Really short.* We're talking a single crisp eyeful here at most.

Immediacy

Your Touchstone cuts right to the chase. You're no longer selling yourself or your commodity. You're simply laying out the facts and letting the customers see the value for themselves. If your offer is strong enough, you don't need to pitch it. When you make an Irresistible Offer, you've made the transition from annoying salesman to trusted friend offering something of desirable value. The customer either wants it or not. If they don't, you just saved yourself and the customer a lot of time by simply moving on to the next prospect.

Now, here's another critical distinction to understand. The offer presented in your Touchstone is usually *separate* from your Core High ROI Offer. More often than not, they are two different entities.

Three of the Greatest Touchstones in History

Let's use Domino's, Columbia House (you know, the place that puts the compact disc ads in TV Guide and other magazines), and Federal Express as examples.

Domino's Pizza

The Touchstone—"Pizza hot and fresh to your door in 30 minutes . . . or less . . . or it's free"—is one of the best ever created.

But it doesn't say anything about the quality of the pizza. And, in the company's early days, that was just as well.

The Touchstone communicated three of the four important ideas beautifully.

Here's what we're selling—fast pizza.

Here's what's in it for you—pizza immediately when you're hungry, or a free pizza.

Here's why you should trust us—if we don't keep our promise, you've got a free dinner.

So, is there a high ROI offer? No. Because, in the beginning, Domino's wasn't offering a great pizza for a fair price. It was fast, but it wasn't a great return on investment for the customer seeking a good-tasting pizza.

The Touchstone was the spark, but it took a High ROI Offer (a better pizza for a good price) to keep the flames blazing over the long run.

Columbia House Records

The Touchstone—"10 CDs for 1 Cent"—is a good one. So good, in fact, that a variation of it has been used by numerous CD and book clubs for many years—and is still used today.

 TIP: Persistent marketing is good marketing. If you see an ad appear again and again over time, by the sheer economics of it, it is most likely very effective marketing. Poor marketing doesn't last long, because the money earned from it will dry up and the campaign can not be sustained.

For anyone interested in the science of marketing, this approach is really interesting. On the surface, it communicates three of the Big Four points beautifully. Then, it gets you halfway there toward the final hurdle . . . and stops. That's because there's a catch to this Touchstone.

Here's what we're selling—cheap compact discs.

Here's how much it will cost you—one penny.

Here's what's in it for you—cheap music.

Here's why you should trust us—hey, what do you have to lose? (It's a low risk, but it still leaves the consumer skeptical—and justifiably so.)

So, what's the high ROI offer? As you might imagine, it's not really 10 CDs for a single penny. You must agree to purchase a subsequent number of CDs at a higher price.

Still, when you consider the total price you'll pay over the length of the agreement, match it up against the number of CDs you receive and the convenience of not having to go to the mall to buy them, you realize you're getting a pretty good deal just the same.

What's the lesson to be gained from the Columbia House example? Having a High ROI offer at the core allows a company to use a certain degree of gimmickry and still stand up to further scrutiny.

There's another example I want to highlight in which—unlike Domino's and Columbia House, which offers cheap pizza and cheap CDs, respectively—a company uses a Touchstone that doesn't talk about price *at all*.

Federal Express

The Touchstone—"When it absolutely, positively has to be there overnight"—doesn't really look like it fits the criteria of The Irresistible Offer Touchstone, does it? It wouldn't seem on the surface to have any particular cachet at all. But it's actually one of the best touchstones ever written.

Let's break it down:

Here's what we're selling—overnight delivery.

Here's how much—we're not saying, but we think this service is so valuable to you, that you probably don't care about the price.

Here's what's in it for you—your delivery is made overnight, and your ass is out of a sling when your project gets there on time.

Here's why you should trust us—for God's sake, how can you have a more trustworthy name than "Federal Express."

45

Nonverbal Communication

As you master The Irresistible Offer you'll come to realize that you can use more than mere words to address the Big Four Questions.

As you can see in the case of Federal Express, the issue of trust is nailed beautifully with the name of the company itself. As they develop more brand equity and reputation, the question is addressed in yet another way again.

Remember that information is transmitted in many ways. It can take the form of an image. It can take the form of the position of your brand in the market place (perhaps one of the subtlest yet most powerful forms of communication in existence—making books by Ries and Trout required reading, especially *Positioning*). It can even take the form of who is doing the selling (choose your sales and customer care reps wisely!).

This Touchstone gives you 75 percent of the High ROI Offer—everything but the price. Of course, if the price were too high, they would be out of business. The point is, though, that they didn't have to deviate too far from the High ROI Offer in creating their Touchstone because Federal Express offers a pretty straightforward product.

You probably won't be so lucky as to have that kind of simplicity.

BELIEVABILITY

What if I offered you $1,000 for every dollar you gave me?

After all, that's one damn powerful Touchstone. Would you take me up on it?

Okay, I don't have to be a psychic to know that you'd be wondering what kind of scam I was trying to pull on you.

There's an often-told story about a direct marketer named Mike Enlow who put this very offer in a newspaper ad to prove a point. He didn't get a single response. Not one.

And that was his point.

The bigger and bolder you make your Touchstone, the more difficult it is to prove, and the harder you have to work to sell your believability and your credibility.

MAGIC FORMULAS FOR BELIEVABILITY

How is believability communicated? How do you prove to your consumer that you can be trusted, and that your offer is *not* too good to be true.

Of course, each case presents its own challenges, but here are a few methods you should consider. Tailor your approach as needed to fit you, your offer, and your customer. Remember, it's good to be bold, but the bolder you are, the higher you raise the bar on making yourself believable.

Proof

There are three types of proof you can use to bolster the credibility of your offer.

There's *social* proof. This is generally provided through testimonials, demonstrating that there are people out there who have tried the product and are quite happy about it. A good testimonial has to have something to prove that you're not just making it up—an e-mail address, a web address, a photo. If you want to say that Marilyn from Cincinnati loves your service, then you'd better demonstrate that Marilyn is a real flesh-and-blood person and not a product of your marketing imagination.

There's *technical* proof. Has the effectiveness of your product been scientifically validated? Do you have some tests that show that your product will actually achieve its stated purpose? Again, these pieces of evidence must be presented in a believable way, or you will undermine your credibility rather than enhance it.

And then there's simply *factual* proof. When you're offering a product, do you have research that shows how the value or popularity of comparable products have increased over time? Businesses that sell merchandise based on precious commodities do this frequently, and with great effectiveness, showing how such products can be good investments.

Credibility

Credibility is all about you. Can you be trusted? Do you have the authority to make your offer believable and desirable? Credibility can take many forms.

Endorsements

Do you have any celebrities or highly regarded authorities who could vouch for your product? People just seem to give more credence to an offer that is backed by someone they've seen on television or read about in the papers. Make sure, though, that the celebrity is appropriate for the product or service you're selling. You wouldn't, for example, hire Michael Jackson to endorse your child day care center. That's an extreme case, but you get the point.

A real-world example that is not quite so extreme can be found in Martin Sheen (a great actor who played the president of the United States on a popular TV show). He was the spokesman for an antiwar commercial before the U.S. invasion of Iraq. The effect of this was quite the opposite of what was intended. People felt their intelligence was insulted (and rightfully so) when a man who plays the president on TV, but who has no political experience himself, was lecturing us on the effectiveness of weapons inspection programs.

Clearly, the creators of the particular piece of propaganda were attempting to use his fantasy-world authority as leverage, but it backfired.

High Profile Customers

If you can say that every employee at IBM or Microsoft or Sony uses one of your products, that makes a pretty compelling case to future customers. If people who have achieved a reputation for success and excellence choose to become your customer, that's a credibility builder that will go far with your target prospects.

Qualifications

Virtually every profession or career field has some association or organization that certifies the quality of its members' work. You should look into that, and also don't forget to cite relevant degrees or credits that speak to your expertise and knowledge.

Awards and Recognition

Has anyone ever taken notice of your work? Have you won any industry competitions? Potential buyers and customers gravitate toward an offer that has a winner's aura. I wouldn't recommend leading with this, though, since it will seem like bragging.

Logic

Don't underestimate the power of appealing to your customers' logical thinking. As you make your offer, their mental wheels are turning. How, they are asking themselves, can you make such a great offer? If you can give them a logical answer to that question, you've moved much closer to the finish line.

There is a cosmetics company in Korea which claims that all of its products cost the U.S. equivalent of $10 or less. It makes you skeptical, right? How could a halfway-decent product cost so little?

But then they explain it, and logic kicks in to great effect.

The company points out that, in cosmetics, 90 percent of the cost is advertising. You're not paying us for a big brand that runs full page ads in *Vogue*, so our costs are significantly lower. Also, they add, most cosmetics products are filler and foam. This adds to the cost and reduces the amount of usable product.

After presenting this logic, their offer goes from unbelievable to highly credible. And, apparently, their stores are jam-packed with eager customers on a regular basis.

It helps that Korean consumers tend to be highly price-conscious, so this offer is well-planned and well-executed.

Keep in mind the logic that can lend credence to The Irresistible Offer. Pointing out to your customers facts like "I have excess stock and must liquidate" or "I have a new source in Asia that can sell to me extremely cheap" provides a powerful rationale for customers to jump at your offer.

Of course, make your claim believable. Sometimes, marketers concoct the lamest stories to boost sales, and the effect is the reverse of what's intended. Let's not let that happen to you.

PUTTING IT ALL TOGETHER

Let's take a look at the way this will actually play out in a marketing campaign, from both your customer's perspective as well as your own.

The Irresistible Offer Creation Process: *What You Do, in Chronological Order*

First Step: Develop a High ROI Offer

Before you do anything else, you create something that provides an obvious Return on Investment for the customer. If you don't do this, there's no point in going any farther (or in staying in business).

Second Step: Create a Compelling Touchstone

You develop the core of your marketing campaign. All of your marketing efforts stay consistent and true to this core. This is the one brand-identifying message you always want associated with your business.

Third Step: Believability

To give your offer and your campaign lasting resonance, you center your business around various believability factors to increase trust. Remember, they're not all verbal.

The Irresistible Offer Sales Process: *What Your Customer Sees,
in Chronological Order*

First Look: Your Touchstone

This piques his interest. Two or three of his big questions
are answered in a way that intrigues and excites him, so
he's willing to dig further to see what you have.

Second Look: Believability

He discovers enough about you and/or your products and
services to know that you can be trusted. This empowers
him to dig deeper.

Third Look: High ROI Offer

If your customer gets to this point and finds that your
touchstone has truly captured the spirit of what you're actually offering, you've got a sale. Better still: If he discovers it's better than what he expected consider your sale a
true slam-dunk.

CONCLUSION

Remember, your marketing has to cut through the nonstop
barrage of marketing nonsense with which your customers
are battered throughout their day.

That's the purpose of an effective Touchstone. Immediately, you present a short, interesting, credible offer to
your prospect that transcends all of the other noise in the
environment.

The customer's Unspoken Inner Dialogue kicks in. It says, "Hey, that's not the normal manipulative advertising claptrap. These guys might actually understand what I want."

You then add in the factors that bolster your Believability.

The Unspoken Inner Dialogue is heard from again. It says, "Okay, this is a great offer, and these guys seem credible. But sometimes nothing is as it seems. What's the real deal? What's the catch here?"

And this is when you're at the make-or-break point: when the Touchstone meets the Offer, and your customer decides whether the reality is equal to the promise. And, sometimes, there is a catch. If your Touchstone is a loss leader, sometimes you may require a bit more from your customer in exchange for the killer deal.

But, after digging deeper, if the prospect finds a truly High ROI Offer at the core, the sale is closed.

CHAPTER 7

The Great Formula

Bringing The Irresistible Offer to a Thirsty Crowd and Selling Them a Second Glass

You too can have business success beyond your wildest expectation—and you don't have to get an MBA or buy a mountain of business books to do it. There's a simple formula—let's call it The Great Formula, because it's so unfailingly effective—that will bring you a steady flow of repeat business from eager customers.

It really isn't any harder than following these three steps:

1. Create *The Irresistible Offer*
2. Present It to a *Thirsty Crowd*
3. Sell Them a *Second Glass*

If you can remember this formula and stick to it, your success is guaranteed. Sure, keep improving your business education and acquire new knowledge, but just remember, whatever you learn is just icing on the cake that is represented by this three-step formula.

Whether you're working to be a better marketer or to write more attractive ad copy, just remember that whatever you learn cannot be a replacement for The Great Formula.

Let's take a closer look at the three steps.

STEP 1: CREATE THE IRRESISTIBLE OFFER

We've covered this pretty extensively in the preceding pages. You *know* how to create The Irresistible Offer. It's a simple concept, but. . . .

Don't Take It for Granted!

Make sure you master the creation of The Irresistible Offer before doing anything else. If you try to move onto Steps 2 and 3 before mastering this basic, fundamental first step, your ultimate success will only be a small fraction of what it could be.

STEP 2: PRESENT IT TO A THIRSTY CROWD

Let's say you're selling new arthritis medications to senior citizens. Are you going to advertise your product on MTV, amidst the heavy metal bands with tattoos and nose rings?

Are you going to market on the Disney Channel to cartoon-happy kids?

Of course not. You can create the world's greatest offer, but if you don't present it to people who have a natural interest, a genuine *hunger*, for your product, you've wasted your time.

Present your offer to people who are interested. *Any point of contact* with your potential customer will work, and many of them will cost you nothing.

You may be asking at this point, what do I present to my customers? How do I present it to them?

I don't need to expand on that for you, because you already know the answers to these questions. The preceding chapters told you how to construct and present The Irresistible Offer. That's your message. All you have to decide on is the audience and the delivery vehicle. Because The Irresistible Offer is so powerful and so compact, it should be the center of every one of your customer-acquisition campaigns.

There are a million ways to get your message out there and just as many books and videotapes on the subject. Just remember, though: If you don't utilize The Great Formula, all of the marketing gimmicks in the world will not reach anywhere near their full potential.

Keep your eye on your own personal advertising ROI. Track and test the effectiveness of your campaigns as much

Points of Contact

One of the most useful marketing constructs I have ever been introduced to is that of customer Points of Contact. If you realize that marketing not only can, but does occur (whether you like it or not) at every point of contact with your customer or potential customer, your mind opens up to some interesting possibilities.

This kind of thinking allowed many of my companies to dramatically increase their profits.

For example, when you make a purchase online, generally once the transaction is complete you are presented with a rather clinical-looking receipt. I used to do that, too, until I applied this construct.

We added something I called a One-Click-Upsell at the back end of each sale of any of our business e-books. We told our customers that all they had to do was click "yes!" and they would get a free month of one of our services for free. No obligation. Billing would start after 30 days.

A startling 45 percent of our customers took us up on this offer. You can imagine the impact on our bottom line.

After this success, I began looking for these opportunities everywhere. One by one, I started finding little marketing opportunities. For example, when we sent out receipts we'd include them with a little note from a Customer Care rep recommending another book. A few days later, we'd hit them with a follow up asking if they had any questions, making sure they were happy with the purchase. We'd also, of course, slip in an appropriate recommendation for another high-quality product.

Just start thinking like this: When do you have the eyeballs of your customers or potential customers?

Smart companies with delivery trucks will wrap their delivery vans with advertising. How much more does it cost them to get this extra exposure? No more than the cost of painting their trucks.

Be sure, however, in all cases that you include a direct response mechanism of some sort—preferably a memorable Web address. Customers probably won't remember your phone number (unless you have something like 1-800-FLOWERS), but they will remember "Flowers Overnight.com."

Always make it clear how you want your customer to respond.

Many brand marketers will tell you it's not necessary to specify a response mechanism in your ads, but isn't it possible that you can further your brand *and* get direct response at the same time? Of course it is. Even if you merchandise your products through common stores, you may want to tell customers what stores to go to, or at least how to find a Web site to learn more about your product—always tell customers *something*.

as possible. You need to know what's working and what's not, rather than just scatter-shooting without a plan.

Be bold. Be aggressive.

Experiment like crazy.

Jettison what's not working.

And then, do more of what is working—to the people who will be receptive to what you're offering.

It's not anymore complicated than that.

STEP 3: SELL THEM A SECOND GLASS

This is where you'll make most of your profit.

It's an undeniable fact, proven over and over again: The cost of selling to an existing customer is far less than the cost of acquiring a new one. Granted, The Irresistible Offer will cut your customer acquisition costs tremendously, but your ROI on existing customers will even outshine that.

McDonald's spends tens of millions of dollars to get new customers in the door to buy a hamburger. McDonald's loses money on that first 89 cent hamburger when contrasted to the fortune they've pumped into advertising and marketing. But once you're there, they make it easy for you to spend money on Cokes, on french fries, on apple pies, on McFlurries, and they know you'll keep coming back.

Paralysis by Analysis

Sometimes people get so wrapped up in testing and tracking that they stop doing the one thing on which they should always spend more of their time: marketing!

This is paralysis by analysis. You get so deep into the process of analyzing things that you simply stop functioning.

Testing and tracking are vital, but unfortunately most businesses don't understand how to do them properly, or how to manage them practically.

Testing is especially important if you're about to risk a large sum of money on a campaign. It can help you discover whether or not your investment will render a positive or negative ROI. And even marketing that has little or no financial risk still risks your most valuable asset: your time.

However, I've heard some test-happy marketing experts tell you that you should test everything. Obviously, this isn't even close to being possible. Every single word of your ad copy can in fact make a difference, but are you going to test every one of them? Of course, that's simply not practical.

What you need is to identify the elements of your copy that are most likely to have the biggest impact on your sales.

For example, old-school direct marketing copywriting geniuses like Joe Sugarman, Gary Bencivenga, Gary Halbert, and Ted Nicholas will tell you that when preparing a direct mail campaign you should test your headline and your order form before anything else.

Why?

(Continued)

61

Paralysis by Analysis *(Continued)*

Because they know that testing these elements is most likely to render the greatest impact on your marketing. Think about it—if people don't get past your headline, does it matter how brilliant the rest of your salesletter is?

Every marketing campaign has a few elements that are more likely to impact your results than the others.

If you're good, and you have the time, you can start refining your techniques and testing the odd thing here and there. For example, I once discovered that the proper use of a check box on an Internet order form increases sales by 36 percent. My good friend Gary Halbert discovered that the city from which you mail a direct marketing piece can have a huge impact on sales as well.

Who'd have thought that!? Keep in mind that these were tests conducted by seasoned marketers who had already tested the basics of their campaigns.

Although discoveries like these are extremely useful, I wouldn't advise a novice to start testing oddball theories on a lark. This kind of thinking, while useful, is also very dangerous because it can lead to paralysis by analysis if you get too caught up in the testing process.

So, identify which elements of your marketing will render the greatest impact, test those, and roll out your campaign with ferocious enthusiasm.

If you're rendering even a tiny ROI, all you have to do is increase your spending to earn more money! Think about that. . . .

They cross-sell and upsell you like crazy while you're there ("You want fries with that?"), and they get you coming back because the food tastes good, it's cheap, it's extremely convenient, it's lightning fast, and it is consistent every single time (you always get what you expect).

People who truly understand the Second Glass concept aren't afraid of losing money to acquire new customers because they understand they'll make major profits in the long run. This is called the "Loss Leader technique." You take a temporary loss acquiring a new customer, knowing that you can come back to that group of customers again and again, and reap great gains.

Embracing this concept gives you great freedom in creating The Irresistible Offer. If you can feel comfortable about losing money on your initial offer, without getting queasy at the thought, it makes the job of creating a High ROI Offer and a powerful Touchstone that much easier.

In fact, being up front about your use of a Loss Leader can make your job of achieving Believability that much easier.

There is a great marketing campaign for computer learning CDs from "Video Professor." The offer includes a free Windows learning CD program to anyone who watches the television commercials. You believe this offer because the company tells you straight up, "I can give this away for free because I know you will be so happy with the result that you'll come back to us for all of your computer learning needs."

 WARNING: Use the Loss Leader strategy *only* if you're absolutely confident of your ability to bring your customer back for additional sales. There's a word for giving away your product for free and absorbing significant losses if you're not sure your customer is coming back. It's called "recklessness." Many businesses have launched into loss-leader campaigns with foolhardy confidence that they can simply create an upsell later. Reckless, indeed.

It's perfect! In a mere 30-second commercial, believability is burned into the buyer's decision-making mind.

In fact, I would even make sure that you have your second offer ready to go immediately. Sometimes, the easiest time to offer a second helping is right after you have consummated the first sale. You've got the customer in the buying mood, so why not go back for more?

Here are some great techniques that can be used any time after the first sale, sometimes the instant the first sale is completed.

SECOND GLASS DELIVERY TECHNIQUES

It's easy to pay lip service to the virtues of selling the Second Glass, but most businesses simply don't do it, and this is one of the primary reasons they fail.

With just a tiny bit of imagination, you can squeeze vast sums in extra profit out of your business, just by selling that second glass. Here's how.

The Upsell

If you're selling a small version of a product, customers may very well be interested in a large. If they're buying "Light," why not offer them the "Deluxe" instead?

If the offer for the Super Sized version of your product is just as irresistible as the original product, it shouldn't be overly difficult to turn a $10 sale into a $100 sale.

Just don't abuse this approach. If you upsell customers crap—products or services that don't offer a higher ROI for the money they're laying out—they're gone forever. All efforts to regain your credibility will be in vain.

The Cross-Sell

If you're selling horses, wouldn't your customers also be interested in saddles? If you are a dentist and you perform a teeth cleaning, wouldn't the same customer possibly be interested in teeth whitening?

The approach obviously needs to be careful here, lest you insult your customer. "Oh, so you think my teeth are ugly?" Overly aggressive or insulting upsells are customer-repellent. They might get an initial sale if the snake doing the pushing is clever, but the customer will associate so much pain with the process that he will avoid coming back. A dentist who stacks emotional pain with the physical pain built in to the office visits is sure to leave a lasting impression on the customer!

Home electronics stores have become masters of the cross-sell. If you're shelling out the money for a big screen TV, they can easily convince you that, once you've made that initial investment, you ought to spend a little more to get the right cables and other accessories to ensure a perfect picture.

Such cross-sell offers can increase your profit-per-sale dramatically.

Think about it. If you make 1,000 sales a month and just add a $1 in profit on accessories and add-ons, that's an extra $12,000 in profit per year.

If the cross-sells are legitimately helping the customer to get a better result, he won't feel that you pitched him. He'll feel that you helped him! Huge difference here. Helping customers not only renders more sales, but also stimulates positive word of mouth (more on that shortly).

The Follow-Up

The two methods mentioned above can be used immediately at the point of sale. Just make sure you do your cross-sells and upsells *after* the first sale is consummated. If you overload your customer with options before the deal is sealed, you may just confuse them right out the door. Have you ever put two bones in front of a dog? What does he do? He is so confused that he doesn't bury either of them. He simply can't commit because he has too many options. Humans, whether we care to admit it or not, are just as easily confused.

Keep it simple.

The Follow-Up Sale is one that occurs any time thereafter.

It may be a day later. It may be a year later.

See "How to Keep the Door Open" later in this chapter for some ideas.

Continuity

Some products just lend themselves to a natural Second Glass. For example, a subscription to a monthly magazine is, in itself, a Second, a Third, a Fourth, and so on.

Continuity products are those that are offered to the customer on a regular basis. They are, in essence, built-in, guaranteed repeat sales.

You may not have heard the name Guthy-Renker, but you've no doubt seen their infomercials. They're one of the world's leading television infomercial marketers. An insider there told me that they no longer even consider taking on new products that aren't continuity-based.

For example, Guthy-Renker sells a superb skin care line that comes with a discount for automatic monthly refills. The product works very well—it has a high ROI ("you invest some money, we give you beautiful skin")—and therefore people are happily paying for it month after month. They get the customer to commit to monthly payments to keep them on board. It's a bit aggressive, but if you're offering a product that works and is reasonably priced, then continuity is doable and leads to perpetual profits.

Overdeliver on every helping, and you'll sell more and more. Here are a few ideas for keeping your customer coming back for more that may spark your imagination.

SECOND GLASS RECIPES

You understand now, on a conceptual level, how the Second Glass is delivered. If I were you, I would spend most of my time thinking at the conceptual level so you can break away from what other people are doing and create bold, never-before-seen marketing tactics.

However, what follows are some specific real-world recipes that break the conceptual down to the actual. These should stimulate your mind to think of even more possibilities.

I challenge you to write down any ideas you come up with as you read, and immediately implement them when you put this book down.

Education

Do your customers know how to use your product? Do they want to learn how to use it better? If they purchased flower seeds from you, would they be interested in a gardening class? Camera stores have made great profits by selling photography classes to people who have bought new Nikons and Canons.

Flip this up, and you have a great customer acquisition tool. Offer free beginning photography classes to people who give you their contact info, and after the class you can sell them on a number of things.

Consulting and Service

Most people aren't really buying your product. They're buying the results they hope to gain from it. You can offer the expert consulting that will help get them the result they desire. Computer sellers do well by selling equipment packages, and then offering the consulting services to come in to set up everything and get it working properly.

Package Deals

What if you bundled your product together with a number of related products that would attract a natural interest?

That's easy money. You can create bundles of almost any variety to squeeze in a few extra sales. Just make sure it's still a High ROI Offer, lest your customer may end up feeling suckered.

Insurance and Warranties

When's the last time you saw an insurance company go out of business because of revenue shortfalls? It doesn't happen. Why? Because they do their homework and have actuaries who can calculate the probable payouts during the year, enabling them to set the appropriate price points and conditions for your insurance policies. This makes profits a statistical certainty.

There are companies that specialize in creating warranty programs for products. Find one, strike up a deal, and open up a new profit stream for yourself.

Logical Additions

Use your imagination. Put yourself in the customers' shoes. If they have just bought your product, what else could they

The reliability of statistics is also an argument for doing your market testing. If you can statistically prove that a particular marketing campaign will render a strong, continuing ROI for you, you've got yourself a license to print money.

possibly need? If you're selling pizza, they may want some sodas. If you're selling tequila, wouldn't they want some limes and salt? If you're selling cameras, they might be interested in a zoom lens. If you're selling a suit, most buyers want some tailoring to achieve that perfect fit.

Side note: These logical additions can become part of your High ROI Offer. In fact, you may want to give one of these things away for free to increase your customer's return on their investment, and keep them coming back for more. Give it away as an unadvertised surprise bonus after the sale and you're sure to make an impression. Imagine getting a free gift, no strings attached, a week after a purchase. Another twist: use that gift to get them back in the store and your generosity may just render more sales.)

Referrals

Maybe you don't have any additional products to offer. But perhaps your business counterparts do. If you sell haircuts, find a company that sells shampoo and strike a deal with them—sell some of their shampoo to your customers for a piece of the profits. Just remember, though, don't forget your core business. Don't get so caught up in these referral deals that you dilute the clarity of your own Touchstone. Remember your own identity.

HOW TO KEEP THE DOOR OPEN

Just remember that it's up to you to preserve a prosperous link between yourself and your customer. The ways to do so are limited only by your own imagination.

Remember "Points of Contact?"

Keep in mind, though, that no one wants to be pummeled over and over again by sales offers. If you keep pitching people repeatedly, they will inevitably tune you out. There are other actions you can and should undertake, though, to keep yourself prominent in your customer's awareness.

Thank You Cards

> *Dear Mark, just a quick card to say how much I enjoyed meeting you the other day and how much I appreciate your business. . . .*

Customers like to be appreciated. Send a thank you for their business and check up on them to make sure they're happy with what you sold them. Give them a reason to stop by your office, and then you have the opportunity to sell them a Second Glass.

Another approach: Give them a Gift Voucher they can give away to a friend.

Birthday Cards

> **Happy Birthday! Stop by our office for a free _____.**

This brings a smile to your customers' face. It makes them think positively about you, and you can offer them the opportunity to stop by your office for a free gift.

Just make sure it's a real gift. If it's a cheap piece of garbage, they'll be more insulted than impressed, and you'll have destroyed all of the good will you built up.

Service Due Reminders

> It's been six months since you last had your teeth cleaned. As you know, a cleaning every six months will prevent tooth decay, will keep your smile sexy and bright . . .

Smart doctors, dentists, and car mechanics are masters of this approach. People respond to reminders that routine service—whether it's for your body or your car—is due.

Some people own items that need servicing and don't even realize it. For example, old video cassette players needed head tightening from time to time to keep the play-back quality at it's peak. Include a little valuable education with your reminder, and you've got a slam dunk.

Newsletters

This is one of my favorite approaches. We live in an in-formation society. On a regular basis, you can deliver information that is of high interest and value to your customers, and then use that newsletter vehicle every now and then to present an Irresistible Offer for a Second Glass.

Like all of these approaches, just make sure what you're delivering is truly valuable. This is the key difference that will prevent your messages from being perceived as junk mail: value and usefulness.

Special Events

On October 31st, do you want to wear a costume that is guaranteed to have everyone raving about you? Come out on October 15th for our annual *free* Ultimate Halloween Costume Design Party.

Come out on February 1st for our *free class*: How to Give Your Lover a Valentines Day that Will Make Them Fall in Love with You Forever. We'll teach you the three things you must do this Valentine's Day that will ensure your lover is reeling in bliss for days.

The other day, I received a postcard from a service station near by to come in for their Grand Opening and get a free coffee, a donut, and a handy pocket-size tire pressure gauge. They hadn't just opened recently. Actually, they'd

Freebie Marketing Tips:

The Golden Rule of Freebies: *Never* give away anything that you couldn't otherwise sell. (Free junk is still junk.)

The Target, Tie-In, Collect Formula

1. Make sure your freebie is *targeted* to the proper audience. Don't give away a free tea-cozy to the guy who just bought a new transmission.

2. Make sure that you *tie-in* the freebie itself somehow to your marketing process. That is, the use of the freebie should lead them further along the marketing process. This can be as simple as including your contact information stenciled on the freebie.

3. Make sure you always *collect* the contact information of the people to whom you are giving the freebie and get their permission to contact them in the future.

Following this formula will multiply the results of your marketing efforts many times over.

only done a little remodeling. But it presented a great excuse to put on a special event and get customers inside the door for additional sales and relationship building.

I didn't go, but if they were smart, they would have included some unexpected gifts, some education, some ways to remember them (the pressure-gauge better have had their contact information printed on it), and coupons for discounts on future service.

Again, be creative. Contacting customers time and time again for a straight sales pitch will wear them out and convert your lucrative client into a cold prospect.

When you use any of the above techniques to capture your customer's interest again, just be sure that each of these approaches is seen as a High ROI Offer in itself. If they can see through it as a thinly veiled sales pitch, then your work has been counterproductive.

Your creativity and determination to keep your customer coming back for a Second Glass will keep you in business for a very long time.

CHAPTER 8

Offer Intensifiers

How to Turn Your Great Product into a Gotta-Have-It-Now Commodity

Offer Intensifiers are devices that will boost an offer's effectiveness—sometimes in the extreme.

You'll find that many of the greatest Touchstones have Offer Intensifiers built right in. When they're used in a believable way (don't fling them about like a used-car-salesmen), they can have a very pronounced and measurable effect.

Just remember again not get ahead of yourself. When crafting The Irresistible Offer, start with your High ROI offer first, and then move toward these steps to intensify it.

Don't limit your use of these devices to your creation of The Irresistible Offer, though. They will also provide oomph to almost any marketing campaign.

URGENCY (CONTRIVED AND GENUINE)

I only make this offer to new customers in the first 48 hours after we've met! . . .

An expiring offer creates urgency in the mind of the customer. If your prospect fears that he won't be able to get an offer if he hesitates, you've successfully eliminated the natural tendency to procrastinate that can keep sales on ice for far too long.

Why do you think that the home shopping networks on television use that digital clock ticking away the seconds at the bottom of the screen? They want buyers to be fully aware that this once-in-a-lifetime offer will slip away if they don't act *now*.

This urgency can be *genuine*. Maybe you are offering something that won't be available again for a long time. In this case, you would be seriously remiss if you didn't point this out to your customer.

Or the urgency can be *contrived*, conjured up by your marketing imagination. We won't get into the ethics of this here. That's a whole discussion for another book. But remember that even contrived urgency can be present in an up-front way to the customer, thereby adding to your effectiveness. You could say, for example, "I won't offer this to you 48 hours from now. Not because I can't, but because I only like to do business with decisive people."

Just make sure that you actually live up to that promise, or you'll lose credibility, and the next time you use that device on a customer it will not be taken seriously (remember "The Boy Who Cried Wolf"?).

Marketing legend Joe Sugarman gave a great example of this once when he spoke at one of my seminars. He used a very deliberately contrived urgency mechanism, and when someone in the auditorium tried to take him up on his offer after the time period was up, Joe gave him a healthy dose of verbal abuse.

He did it humorously, of course. But the point was made. And we all learned the value of using urgency as an effective sales device.

We also learned that next time Joe says, "in the next two minutes" he's not kidding, so we'll all react a lot faster to his offers.

ADDED VALUE

Stack on some unexpected added value to your offer, and your customer will resist less and less. This is best included as part of your closing process. Think of a bonus you can add to the deal to make it seem all the sweeter. Just be sure to offer something of genuine value. Remember the Golden

Rule of freebies: Never give anything away that you wouldn't otherwise be able to sell.

RISK REVERSAL

I'd say this is a good idea, but it's more than that. It's absolutely essential. The most daunting obstacle standing in the way of making a sale is your buyer's fear of risk. If you remove the risk of doing business with you, you've cleared the way for a favorable decision.

Domino's, for example, removed all of the risk right up front. If our pizza arrives late, you don't have to pay for it.

At the very least, you should *always* back up every offer with a money-back guarantee. I'm always surprised at the number of business people who won't do this because they're afraid of people taking advantage of them.

If you don't offer money-back guarantees with your offers, you will begin doing so immediately once you learn the following facts:

1. Most people will not take you up on a money-back guarantee, even if they are extremely unsatisfied. (Thank you, Joe Vitale, for first teaching me this.)
2. Any refunds you have to give will be greatly outweighed by your increased sales caused by your risk reversal.
3. You are required by law in the United States to refund a purchase in the first 30 days if a customer

is not satisfied. Many other countries have similar laws.

4. If you have The Irresistible Offer, by definition very few people will ever ask you for a refund because they'll be delighted with what you have sold them.

Get creative with your risk reversal ideas. If you can remove your customer's fear about doing business with you, you're going to have a steady flow of new and repeat business.

RISK REVERSAL TACTICS

Again, let's move now from the conceptual to the actual. Feel free to model any of these specific tactics, but be careful not to let them limit your thinking.

If you think "risk reversal" and not "money-back guarantee," your mind immediately opens up to the possibility of other risk-reversal tactics. This way of thinking will leave your competitors gasping for air as they try to figure out how you suddenly became so damn clever.

Money-Back Guarantee

If you are not 100 percent satisfied simply return it to us, and we'll refund the entire purchase price on the spot.

This is the most obvious and common form of risk reversal. It's common because it works extremely well. When

I say "common," though, I mean "common among risk-reversal tactics." The fact is, the majority of businesses don't advertise this out of the fear that their customers will come back and rip them off. You know better now, so you'll easily be able to crush any of your competitors who are still stuck in stone age thinking.

Payment Plans

Pay us only $20 now, and you can take it home today.

If customers only have to put up a small amount now, they tend to perceive the total risk as being lower. Most people don't think too far past that first payment. They are thinking, "Well, it's only $19 right now," even if it's really $19 a month for the next few years.

If you're confident about your product, you can tie this in with a generous return policy for an even more appealing risk reversal.

Loss Leaders

The first one's free.

There's a reason why drug dealers give away free samples.

As you remember from the previous chapter, a loss leader is where the first product you offer your customer is one at such a discount that you're actually losing money on the initial sale, in hopes of making that up and more on the back end. If the loss leader is free or priced so low as to be negligible, there is very little risk for the consumer and therefore you'll tend to get a higher initial response.

I would not recommend this tactic to an amateur or to a company with a cash-flow crunch, because it might take some time to work out every aspect of this approach before it puts you in profits. However, for more experienced and risk-tolerant marketers, it is one of the most powerful weapons in your arsenal.

Drug dealers, one would imagine, are not very clever marketers, but they do have a product so addictive that they know they can lose money on that first freebie because their customers are hooked and will keep coming back.

Let's hope your customers are coming back because it benefits them-but you get the idea.

Warranties

If you have any problems over the next 5 years we will fix it for you at your home for free. 24 hour service guaranteed.

If the product you offer is one such that your consumers are excessively worried about its breaking down, then a warranty may be just the ticket to reverse risk. If they know that all they have to do once it breaks down is call you and you'll send someone out there to fix it on the spot, they have very little to worry about.

Pay for Results

You pay me nothing now. If the ad copy I write for you increases your profits, all I ask is for 10 percent of the increase.

Smart marketing consultants use a pay-for-results system because they are highly confident in their abilities. This is a complete risk reversal for the client. Hey, if he can increase my profits, it would certainly be worth giving him 10 percent. If he can't then I pay him nothing.

If you're highly confident in the effectiveness of your product, and you have a valid way of tracking the results and ensuring that your clients are accountable and trustworthy, this is a great tactic.

Free Support

This is a great tactic for software companies. All too often, we purchase products and don't have a clue how to use them. The companies then leave us in the cold and ask us to pay for support.

Having sold quite a bit of software in my day, I understand that offering free support isn't always a viable revenue model. It's hard to get a one-time payment from customers and then be at their beck and call for years later. How do you pay for that?

If your product is so well put-together that very little support is needed, you can probably safely take this risk.

I sold a large package of software source code a few years ago at a greatly discounted price. The development cost for the code was over $1,000,000, but I sold rights to the code to 2,000 people at $1,000 a pop. A great offer for them, but I knew that it wouldn't make sense for me to support such a massive volume of code for free.

What I did was put together a self-supported user community and a directory of consultants who could support them for a reasonable fee.

The community reversed the risk for many of the purchasers and pushed them further along in their buying decision.

Try Before You Buy

You pay nothing until after you have tried our product for 30 days.

Copywriting legend Gary Halbert said that this is the most powerful tactic he has ever used, but in Gary's words, "Very few people have the balls to test it."

He would ask for people to write in and send him a check and say that he wouldn't cash the check for 30 days until they were sure they are satisfied.

The cold fact is, most people will have forgotten that they even sent you the check, so the risk is far lower than you may even think.

Food for Deeper Thought

Triple your money back!

It may sound crazy, but what if you have a product that works 99 percent of the time? If you give them a triple your money back guarantee, only 1 percent of your customers could ever qualify for it, and only a tiny fraction of that 1 percent will take you up on it. Compare that to the increase in sales the triple-your-money-back offer gives.

If you can't get it to work, I'll personally visit your house and set it up for you.

You'd have to test this to make sure it works, but I bet you'll find that very few people would take you up on this (unless it's something extremely difficult to set up). This would work well for a product that is normally hard to install, but for which you have included a very easy-to-follow installation guide or process.

Hot and fresh to your door in 30 minutes or less or it's free.

Getting the idea? The previous two examples may not be Touchstone-worthy as they stand, but they can certainly increase the intensity of your pitch regardless. Carefully work risk reversal into your Touchstone, and the results, as you know now, can be amazing.

SCARCITY

People love buying things that very few other people can have. That's just human nature, and you can take advantage of it.

People also have a tremendous fear of loss. If your prospects feel that they will lose out if they don't act now, that fear can stimulate an otherwise passive prospect into instant action.

Go to an art auction sometime. The auctioneer will always stress when a particular piece of art is part of a limited, numbered edition. Buyers are more willing to get out their checkbooks for a lithograph that is one of 100 instead of one of an unlimited batch.

Of course, if the piece is a one-of-a-kind original, the scarcity can ramp the value into the millions.

If there is a limited number of what you're offering, the customers feel as if they had better take advantage so that they don't regret it later.

Of course, using this tactic doesn't work with every product. It would be ridiculous, of course, for Domino's to claim they had a limited number of pepperoni pizzas. But jewelers, art dealers, and purveyors of quality photography do it all the time, to great effect.

Ironically, fast food joints do use this tactic on occasion to great effect. Have you ever heard of the McRib? This is an item that McDonald's will run on rare occasion for only weeks at a time. When it returns, McDonald's will boast that the McRib is back for only a limited time. Who cares? Well, a lot of people actually. The sandwich has sort of a cult following and people have dedicated web sites to it!

87

EASE

If it's difficult to do business with you, why would anyone want to be your customer?

Ordering from you should be dead simple. It should require no complex thought, and absolutely no deliberation on how to properly place an order.

Getting answers to pre-sale questions should not be met with any resistance, delay, or evasion.

Your customer should never have to say, "Wow, what a great product! How do I order it?"

One of my early marketing mentors, Joe Vitale, tells a story about how he saw an ad for a guitar called the Tacoma Chief that fired him up so much he wanted to buy one on the spot. He examined the ad and discovered there was no way to contact the company listed at all. No web site. No phone number. No address. Nothing.

He figured they must be banking on people walking in to the local guitar shop, so he broke out the phone book and called around. Only one of the stores had even heard of the guitar. The one that did said they didn't know how to find one.

Joe still doesn't own a Tacoma Chief.

If the company had simply included a web address or a phone number he would have purchased one immediately.

Tip: Walk yourself through your own sales process. Ask yourself honestly: If you were the consumer, how would you feel? Was it as easy as it could be? How can you make it easier? Hire others to do the same for you and get their opinions. Ask them specifically about how easy and pleasant it was.

Smart car salesmen will fill out your sales slip for you while they're talking to you. That's just one less thing you have to do, and it brings you one step closer to the sale.

Anything that adds unnecessary steps or confusion to the sales process has a negative impact on sales. This company went beyond that and asked you to hurdle a 100-foot brick wall at the beginning of the sales process.

PRICING TRICKS

There's a fascinating psychology when it comes to pricing and customer decision making about buying. Some of what you're about to read may seem quite odd and counterintuitive, but I can tell you from experience these tactics are extremely powerful.

Intuitively, we may think that to increase sales with price all you have to do is lower it. The fact is, this doesn't always work. In fact, lower price can actually reduce sales. Read on.

The Law of 7s and 9s

Lowering your prices will not always increase sales, but in certain cases, ending your price in a 7 or a 9 will.

Finding the right combination of numbers can have a huge impact on your business. I once conducted a test where we compared the following prices for a download-able software product:

$97

$99

$95

The $97 price outsold $99 by a factor of two. No surprise there, right? It's two dollars cheaper.

But $97 also outsold $95 by a *factor of five.* Yes, a higher price was *five times more popular* than a lower price.

Think about that—by simply adding two dollars to the price I was able to multiply our sales by 5 times.

The "Law of 7 and 9" is fairly well accepted by most direct marketers, but you should do your own experimentation. Figure out which combination of numbers in your price will yield the greatest sales.

Price Increase for Perceived Value

Significantly increasing the price of a product (whether it ends in a 7 or 9 or not) can increase sales as well.

Robert Cialdini in his classic book *Influence* cites a case where a jewelry store owner left instructions to a clerk to slash all prices in half. Sales were horrible, and he wanted to get rid of the inventory fast. The clerk misunderstood the note and thought the owner was advising him to double the price. So that's what they did.

At the end of the day, the entire inventory was sold out.

The idea here is a higher price created a higher perceived value.

Contrast

A classic direct marketing trick is to compare the price of your product to a higher-priced product or to the "actual value" of the product to make the price seem lower.

This is an incredibly powerful tactic that comes in many flavors.

Car Salesmen and Real Estate Agents when showing you their wares tend to show you the higher-priced models first. Why? These smart salesmen know that when you see the higher-priced models first, you are more likely to purchase a model that is higher in price than you would have accepted if left to your own devices.

Imagine, you're looking at $200,000 Bentleys and Ferraris, and that $60,000 Porsche doesn't seem so expensive anymore.

Direct Marketers have mastered this technique. Well-written salesletters sometimes walk you through the value of what you're about to purchase. They play with your perceptions and get you to expect that the price could very well end up in the thousands.

After reading ad copy like that, you'll see a $397 price tag for a box full of books and tapes and think you're getting a bargain. Without the comparison and contrast, the price would be perceived as much higher.

The device is used copiously in infomercials as well.

How many times have you heard the phase, "How much would you pay now?!"

The infomercial will stack on benefit after benefit and show you how the value of the package gets higher and higher as it goes.

When you see that you're getting $159 worth of products for only $19.97, it's an offer that's really hard to pass up.

The better-educated among us tend to laugh and joke about these tactics, but we are also the ones secretly purchasing these products when no one is looking.

Discounts, Rebates, and Coupons

These tactics are really just additional ways of delivering Contrast.

If the list price of the product is $100, you feel lucky when you get a $20 discount.

The price is still $80, but we perceive that price as a better deal when we get "$20 off."

There are as many ways to employ these tactics as your mind can cook up. Develop a habit of combing through newspapers to see how others are using this tactic effectively. When you go through a retail shop, pay attention there as well. If you put down a newspaper or magazine, or leave a large store, without a new marketing idea you weren't paying attention.

UNIQUENESS—REAL AND PERCEIVED

If your customers believe that they can only get the product they desire from you, then, boom, the sale is made. They want it, and you're the only one who has it.

If you wanted to extend your life by 200 years and there was only one company in the world who offered a viable way to do so, would you buy from them?

I think it's safe to say we'd not only give them our business, but perhaps our life-savings as well.

This is the essence of the Rosser Reeves Unique Selling Proposition. It is extremely powerful. Make your customers believe you are their only source for what they want.

Let's make this clear. It's not critical to actually *be* unique. What's important is to be *perceived* as unique.

Many businesses make the mistake of assuming that everyone knows about their competition. The fact is, the public probably doesn't. They haven't investigated your field very carefully. Even if your competitors are advertising, you can block them out if you center your advertising around a great Touchstone that separates you from them. If you do that, customers are far more likely to notice your approach, and your competitors will remain unnoticed. At that point, you have established the aura of uniqueness.

Be the loudest. Be the best. Have the most compelling Touchstone. Do that and *bang*, you're unique. Or at least, it will seem that way as your prospects' eyes gloss over the ads for your competitors and are drawn to yours.

Here's another way of looking at it. The product you're selling may not be unique, but your use of The Irresistible Offer can make you so.

Domino's certainly wasn't the only player in the pizza game, but they were the only "30 minutes or it's free" guys. They weren't unique, but their ingenuity transformed them into something that was.

BRAND VALUE AND POSITIONING

Much can be said about this, and I heartily recommend you read many of the great books on this topic by Al Ries and Jack Trout.

Here's the most important point in a nutshell: If your product is *perceived* as the best in your industry, you have

multiplied the effectiveness of your marketing efforts exponentially. That's the power of your brand.

For me personally, if I see a piece of clothing from Sal-
vatore Ferragamo I am more likely to look favorably upon
it. Even if Prada (a brand I personally don't look on as favorably) were to come out with a piece of clothing that is
more aesthetically pleasing to my eye, I bet I'd be more
likely to choose the Ferragamo. That's all because of the
way I perceive those two brands.

The power of The Irresistible Offer will multiply itself as
the value of your brand increases. There are many factors
by which we evaluate brands (Wal-Mart offers the best
deals, McDonald's is the fastest, and so on), but the most
powerful of all is the brand's *position.*

The position has nothing to do with who has a certain
quality (best, fastest, cheapest, and so on)—it has everything to do with who is at the top of your mind when you
are looking for a product.

The prime directive in positioning is to be the first one
on the market. Did you realize that, in blind taste tests,
Pepsi is almost always chosen over Coke by consumers?
And yet Coke remains the number one soft drink because it
was on the market first. Blue jean styles have changed more
often than the weather, and yet Levi remains at the top of
the heap because that brand was there first.

It would be safe to say that this phenomenon is due to
the psychological phenomenon known as "primacy." If you

are asked to remember a list of items, you are 10 times more likely to remember the first item on the list than any of the items in the middle.

"Recency" is the flip side of this equation. You are also far more likely to remember the last item in a list over any of the middle items as well.

This is why Coke is still advertising constantly. Their position is securely at the top of our minds, but in order for it to remain so, they have to capitalize on the phenomenon of recency in order to keep it there.

Even if you are not the first on the market, though, aggressive advertising can make it seem as if you were.

I've seen companies knock off brands that created a category. They wiped out the pioneer. How? They just hit the market harder and faster, and did a better job dominating the consumer consciousness. The consumer doesn't even know the pioneer exists, and the better-marketed knockoff overtakes it.

It's like the old joke about two hikers being chased by a man-eating grizzly bear. One of the hikers asked the other, "Are you fast?" And his buddy replied, "I don't have to be fast. I just have to be faster than you." That's the trick here. You don't have to be first on the market. But you do have to be the first one recognized by your customer.

RECOMMENDATIONS

This is the most powerful Offer Intensifier of them all.

Think about it. If someone you know well and respect recommends a product to you, you're much more likely to check it out than if you got that same recommendation from a stranger. This word-of-mouth marketing is so powerful that it cuts through almost any amount of bad advertising.

I've purchased products that friends recommended, even though I had previously written the item off in my mind completely.

Having a High ROI Offer will naturally increase word-of-mouth recommendations.

No, let me rephrase that.

A High ROI Offer is a *prerequisite* to word-of-mouth advertising. It's a fact. People don't recommend crap to their friends.

This is so powerful an Intensifier that you shouldn't leave it to chance. You can accelerate the process. Incentivize the word-of-mouth spread of your marketing message, and watch it catch on like wildfire. You'll need to experiment with various approaches, but I would recommend this as a staple to any marketing plan.

97

Remember, though, your incentive can take any form. It doesn't have to be money. It can be discounts, free service, or any benefit that comes to mind. Play with this. Find a combination that works.

And then crank up the volume and watch your sales explode.

More on this later.

CHAPTER 9

The Offer Continuum

How do you know if your Irresistible Offer is a good one? Can you predict how effective it will be?

It's impossible to answer those questions without testing. It is, however, possible to make some educated guesses. In fact, if you don't have a wise starting point, your testing will most likely be a total waste of time.

I like to think that marketing is *part art, part science, and part magic.*

With well-formed marketing experiments, you can make some pretty reliable predictions about what works and what doesn't. That's the *science* of marketing. These predictions are most reliable when you're doing simple split run testing of one version of an ad against another (assuming you have isolated your variables properly) and you have collected enough data to make a statistically significant observation.

Envisioning and executing campaigns that work is the *art* of marketing. All of the scientific knowledge and testing rigor of the world will be totally unhelpful if your campaigns are simply ineffective. You might be able to prove with statistical certainty that Bad Campaign A is better than Worse Campaign B, but they're still both bad campaigns.

The *magic* of marketing has to do with your own enthusiasm, belief, and confidence affecting your results. This is a topic for another book, but I can say with reasonable certainty that what you expect will in fact have a significant impact on your marketing and your business. If you expect good results, you are more likely to get them. If you expect doom and gloom, they're probably on your horizon. This may sound like hocus pocus to you, but there is evidence for this in the world of science. We know that the expectations of an experimenter can in fact affect the results of an experiment (one of the reasons scientists prefer double blind experimentation).

One of the greatest living scientists, Rupert Sheldrake, has even come up with a name for the transmission medium through which thought and information is passed in a way as yet unexplainable by modern physics: morphogenic fields. He has amassed a large body of data that supports the idea that thought does in fact have an impact on the physical world and especially on living things.

100

With that said, the following tools will allow you to improve your art. That is, these can be used to evaluate any offer and help predict, through pretesting, how effective it will be.

(The science of marketing should be a lifelong study, and the magic of marketing is something you should consciously apply every single day.)

When crafting The Irresistible Offer, use of these tools can have profound and farreaching impact.

HOW TO USE THE OFFER CONTINUUM

What follows is a series of questions you can ask yourself about any offer. This isn't a competition or a scoring system. The idea here is not to get the highest score possible—it's to elicit observation and insight.

Simply use this tool to evaluate your offer as it is. Identify strengths and weaknesses, and then try to step back and take a look at the whole picture.

None of these factors exist in a vacuum.

If, for example, you score very well in some areas, but your price is extremely high, this may not be a problem at all. That is, the higher price may, in fact, help matters for you.

If, however, your price is high and you aren't strong enough in other areas to justify it, you may need to reevaluate your offer.

Also, this exercise will help you in determining the flavor of your Touchstone as well. If, for example, you rank a "10" on the "How Obvious Is the Need?" scale, your Touchstone should come right out and say what you do (among other things).

If the need is not so obvious, you may need to lead with something not so direct. The Touchstone may need to address an underlying problem that the product solves.

Each of these questions will lead to similar extremely useful insights.

See how it works?

Great! Let's get started.

HOW OBVIOUS IS THE NEED?

1 (Totally Obscure) ←——————→ **10 (Totally Obvious)**

In this regard, a company like Federal Express is blessed.

The need is obvious. If you need to get it there overnight, you call FedEx.

How Obvious Is the Need?

If the need for your product is obvious, it pays to let people know what your product is immediately. Why hesitate for a second?

But what if the need is not so obvious?

Maybe you're selling a brand new product that never existed before you invented it. Maybe it's a product that is difficult to explain in a short sentence.

If your need is not obvious on the surface, don't worry. Simply craft your Touchstone in a way that addresses your customer's core needs—the needs that your product will fulfill.

I've got my own example of a product that was not easy to explain to people. One of my old companies (now defunct) was called StartBlaze. It was very hard to say in just a few words what StartBlaze was all about.

At its core, though, what we were offering was web site traffic. We created an effective Touchstone for StartBlaze, and the sales ignited like kindling.

"Give us $1 and we'll send 1,000 people to your web site."

Now, that doesn't explain what StartBlaze did or how it provided services to customers, but it did go right to the heart of what our customers wanted.

HOW GENUINE IS THE NEED?

1 (Doesn't Need It At All) ←————————→ 10 (It's Life or Death)

If your customer doesn't really need what you're offering, you may have a mighty tough road ahead trying to sell it.

At the other extreme, if your customers must have what you're selling, or their lives will be much more difficult without it, then you're coming right out of the gate with an advantage.

If people don't need your product, then they had better really want it. In fact, some marketers go so far as to say, "You don't get rich fulfilling needs. You get rich fulfilling wants."

Andrew Carnegie and Bill Gates may take issue with that, seeing as they both became two of the richest men in the history of the world fulfilling needs.

However, there certainly are a lot of "want" industries, and if you're in one, it may not be so easy to evaluate. In fact, you need to spend your marketing efforts on creating the want or the desire.

For example, it may go without saying that most women in America want a diamond ring from the man asking their hand in marriage. Heck, it may have even crossed over into a need at this point, since not having one will require some explaining, but you see what I mean.

Now, where do you think this desire for a diamond ring came from? Well, obviously it's just a part of our culture, right? I mean, everyone buys a diamond ring for his fiancée, right? It must be an age-old custom.

If you think an age-old custom that dates back to 1940 is age-old then you'd be right. The tradition of giving a ring dates back to Greco-Roman mythology, but it wasn't until De Beers began an advertising campaign in the 1940s that the diamond became the standard. Some even go so far as to say that De Beers not only artificially created this demand, but also artificially manipulates scarcity.

Pretty impressive, isn't it? They created a demand so strong that it became a cultural standard and then cut back the supply so that they could get an even higher price.

What's the point? Well, where need does not exist, you can create desire. If De Beers could do it with diamonds and Gary Dahl could do it for the Pet Rock, is there any limit?

Only in your imagination.

However, unless you're a master at spinning a loom of sales-hypnosis, I'd recommend sticking with solving problems and fulfilling needs.

Now, let's end this with a completely different perspective that may spur some conflicting, but perhaps useful thoughts. Perhaps diamonds and Pet Rocks really do fulfill a need.

One could argue we all need entertainment, and the Pet Rock certainly gave us that. One could also argue that a man needs to flex his monetary muscle in front of his woman. He also may need to communicate clearly to other men, "Hands Off!" Would it be safe to say that a diamond now fulfills that need?

I think it's a totally valid argument, but we have to look back to the question, "How obvious is the solution?" Probably not very obvious for diamonds in the early days, but their marketing sure took care of that.

HOW COMMON IS A SOLUTION FOR THE PROBLEM?

1 (Can Get It Anywhere) ◄————————► **10 (We're the Only One)**

Maybe others are offering similar solutions to the same problems your customers are facing. Don't despair. You're not dead in the water. You just need to figure out ways to differentiate yourself with your Touchstone or work on being perceived as unique.

Remember: if you can be perceived as unique then, for all practical purposes, you are.

CAN YOU DEMONSTRATE A RETURN ON INVESTMENT?

1 (Can't At All) ◄————————► **10** (Quite Easily)

Can you use facts, research, recommendations, charts, and graphs to show your customers that they will easily get a solid return on their investment, a return that greatly outweighs the price you're asking them to pay?

If you can, your chances of success are multiplied.

If you can't, well, all is not lost, but you've got to do a much more intense job of selling.

HOW EMOTIONAL IS YOUR OFFER?

1 (Coma-Inducing) ◄————————► **10** (Strong Men Weep)

Sales increase when you can tie your product or service into an emotional need.

Don't overdo this, please. Too many marketers grab hold of your emotions as though they were roping a steer. They try to convince you that your pet kitten will die and your penis will shrink if you don't jump all over what

107

they're selling. This approach will not render a Second Helping unless the emotional power is justified.

People want to buy a product that makes them feel good, that addresses and eases their fears and insecurities. If you can meet that need, you're on your way to a sale.

If your offer is dry, it doesn't mean that all is lost. You just have to work hard to compensate in other ways.

HOW TIMELY IS YOUR OFFER?

1 (Don't Need It Anytime Soon) ◄————————► **10 (Need It Now Dammit!)**

If your prospects don't need your commodity right now, you'll have to convince them that they do. If you can't provide a compelling reason to buy now, you're going to have a tough time generating sales.

Of course, if your prospect does have a genuine urgent need, and you're well aware of this, then your job of selling just became a lot easier.

When urgency doesn't exist, you can always concoct it out of thin air, and sometimes the result is all the same. (See Chapter 8 on Offer Intensifiers.)

HOW DOES YOURS STACK UP AGAINST KNOWN COMPETITION?

1 (They're Great and We Suck) ◄————————► **10 (We're Clearly the Best)**

Okay, so maybe your product is not the best, on merit, in the marketplace. Don't give up hope just yet.

If you're not the best, you have some options:

1. Improve your product somehow so that you are in fact better, or at least as good, as the competition.
2. Bank on the fact that you can outsmart and outmarket your competitors, and that no one will ever know how much better they are in terms of quality.

Of course, the first option is the best one, but you'd be surprised how many people have achieved a degree of success by following the latter.

Don't forget, though: Long-term success is dependent on a truly High ROI Offer. You may not be the best, but if you're giving the customer a High ROI, that may be good enough.

Now, if you actually are the best in your field and you can prove it, the psychological power of such an argument is incredibly strong. It makes it hard for people to do business with anyone else.

But, you have to market your superiority aggressively. If you're the best, but nobody knows it, you might as well be the worst.

HOW DO YOU COMPARE TO THE KNOWN COMPETITION ON PRICE?

1 (Tiffany Prices) ◄————► 10 (Bargain Rack)

This is not as simple an issue as it appears on the surface. Instinctively, you would assume that if you have the lowest price, you'll be the highest seller.

Not necessarily true.

As we alluded to before, if you're the best, you may be able to charge a little more—maybe even a lot more—for your product.

Let's talk about boutique marketing.

A boutique approach is one in which you position yourself with a superior solution and charge accordingly. The beauty of this approach is that, with fewer customers, you can make more profit with far less hassle. Think about it. If you could make 10 times as much income with one-tenth the number of customers, you've got a much easier life.

Surprisingly, I've found that the customers who are willing to spend more on a product are actually far less trouble, customer for customer, than those who are shopping for a bargain.

A further distinction: If you're the least expensive in terms of price, but your product is crap, you will still have a hard time making a sale. Even cost-conscious buyers want a return on their investment, and they won't buy poor merchandise, no matter how cheap it is.

Remember, you can't even give away a product that you couldn't otherwise sell. Even your freebies need to have high value.

The economics of a buying decision go beyond the surface price. The hidden cost of purchasing an inferior product will outweigh, by many times, any benefit gained by discount pricing.

All of this should be taken into consideration when crafting your offer. Price does, in fact, help, but it does not exist in a vacuum.

CHAPTER 10

Great Offers through History

Three of the greatest examples of The Irresistible Offer have already been discussed in detail: Domino's Pizza, Columbia House Records, and Federal Express.

These three companies are legendary in their success and it's easy to see why.

Here are some less dramatic examples that may not even qualify as The Irresistible Offer. However, they are still great offers in their own right and are certainly worthy of study.

Some are better than others. Some fit the mold completely. Some are simply illustrative as great Touchstones. I challenge you to think about each one and see if it qualifies as The Irresistible Offer.

Analyzing every piece of marketing you see in this way will soon turn you into a Master of the Irresistible Offer.

"BE ALL YOU CAN BE"

The Army has since changed their slogan to "An Army of One" after using "Be All You Can Be" for over 20 years.

I think this was a terrible move and the Army's lagging recruitment statistics back up my sentiment.

After spending more than eight years of my life in the Army I imagine how this probably happened. It's the same thing that happens in the corporate world. Some high-ranking individual who was dangerously out of touch with reality (we joked, "he's so high ranking he's echelons above reality") decided that since the world was changing the Army needed to change its image to keep up with the times.

Be all you can be was one of the greatest marketing campaigns in history, and its persistence proved it. The Army didn't need to change it's slogan—it needed to treat its soldiers better (something they are learning now).

"Be All You Can Be" is a great Touchstone. When you hear those words associated with the Army it immediately puts a powerful offer in your mind.

"Leave your life behind. Come to us and let us mold you. We'll turn you into the best possible person you can be. There is greatness inside of you waiting to be unleashed."

This is a powerful offer for a young person. And I feel the Army actually delivers on this. With all of its flaws, and all of its dangers, the Army did absolutely transform me. (It has ruined many people, too, though. It's all in what you do.)

The point is, with this campaign the Army had all three elements of The Irresistible Offer.

The Army's new campaign makes a High ROI Offer; it has a mediocre Touchstone, but it severely lacks one thing: believability. "An Army of One" sounds like the title to a cheesy Jean-Claude Van Damme movie. "Be All You Can Be" is honest and genuine.

"YOU GIVE US 22 MINUTES. WE'LL GIVE YOU THE WORLD"

WINS Radio in New York offers their listeners something wonderful.

You're in a hurry, but you absolutely must stay up on the times. If you can tune in to these guys on your way to work in the morning, you won't have to waste any more time out of your day. You'll just make your regular morning commute, and you'll walk out of your car with the ability to look like you actually have time to read.

115

Oh, and did I mention this is an advertisement for a news broadcast? No, I didn't, but you already knew that. You knew it the moment you read the Touchstone.

A great Touchstone sometimes *implies* more than it tells. Implying something can be far more powerful than *saying* something outright. Somehow, if your reader has to connect the dots in his own mind about something, the lesson has far more impact.

The great "Two Young Men" direct marketing sales-letter (the most mailed direct marketing piece in history) used year after year by the *Wall Street Journal* employs this tactic. They never say outright that the more successful of the two young men reads the *Wall Street Journal*, but they implied it. There are many who believe that this device of implying is almost solely responsible for the success of the Two Young Men letter.

"WE REPORT. YOU DECIDE."

This is the Touchstone used by Fox News. Stop and ask yourself now what it says to you.

There is a strong feeling by many (and quite justifiably so) that many news agencies are unforgivably biased in their reporting. That is, rather than reporting, they are influencing, which is a cardinal sin for an agency proclaiming to be a source of facts—not opinion.

Of course, one could argue that it's impossible to be completely objective about anything. That is, a report of anything, by definition, is selective. You can't possibly present every bit of information available, so you *must* omit something. In this process of omission, it becomes quite easy to give the appearance that you omitting information that supports one perspective or another—and thus being biased.

Even still, people feel that news agencies have gone too far. It's not just a bias inherent in the process, but a bias that betrays the political leanings of those preparing the news.

To counter this growing sentiment (one especially felt by conservatives in the United States as the news media is seen as largely liberally biased by many). Fox News wanted to present themselves as an objective source of information.

Now, some may argue that to counter the media's liberal bias Fox News is conservatively biased (and they may be right), but one can't argue with the effect of their marketing.

Fox News has unseated the long-time winner in 24-hour cable television news coverage: CNN.

CNN was the only show in town for many years, and they were catapulted to rock-star-level fame when they covered the 1990 Gulf War. Knowing everything we do about branding, CNN should have easily been able to defend their position in the market.

Fox News, armed with a strategic deployment of The Irresistible Offer, however, blew them out of the water.

FANATICAL SUPPORT

This seemingly innocuous Tagline offered by RackSpace Managed Hosting is not so innocuous at all to anyone who has looked for a good managed hosting service for a medium to large web site project.

Most web hosting companies are far from fanatical in their support. Heck, they are downright criminal in their negligence. When a company comes along and says, "It's our mission to support you," you definitely take notice.

Their challenge was that it was very hard to make such a claim believable in an industry full of criminally absent support personnel.

"Believability" for them has been combated by walking their talk. They've proven to me time and again that they actually *are* fanatical in helping their customers.

They are using their sales process to prove that as well. I recently had an experience with them looking to host a new project of mine, and I kept stalling on the deal because of existing obligations.

They asked me, "What is it that's slowing this deal down?" Damn good question. I told them honestly, and they addressed it immediately—earning my business again.

Their reputation and their sales process are providing Believability where it might be hard to show in their marketing. Generally, the more expensive and complicated the process, the tougher your job of establishing Believability will be.

"WE'LL BEAT ANYONE'S ADVERTISED PRICE OR YOUR MATTRESS IS FREEEEEEEEE"

I haven't seen this commercial in over two years, but I still remember it like I saw it yesterday. The annoying voice of Sit 'n Sleep spokesman has found a permanent home in my head.

Sit 'n Sleep is famous in Southern California for this obnoxious and seemingly illogical commercial. I mean, what are they going to do? "Sorry, we can't beat that price, so we're going to have to give it to you for free."

Duh.

Yes, some dismiss this commercial as just annoying sales hype, but you have to ask yourself: Why has this Touchstone not changed for years?

As I have said before, you generally don't see an ineffective marketing campaign repeat itself for very long. If marketing is persistent, it's performing. The economics simply don't support it. This "illogical" commercial must have something going for it.

The Touchstone does in fact communicate one thing clearly: You're guaranteed to get the best price here.

The annoying way in which the message is delivered is so obnoxious that people joke about it all the time.

Yeah, we may joke about it, but we never forget it. And joking about it means *talking* about it. Some may scoff at my inclusion of this campaign in this book, but the campaign has in fact withstood the test of time for over a decade.

"WE WILL HONOR THE LOWEST PRICE YOU CAN FIND FOR UP TO 60 DAYS AFTER YOUR PURCHASE"

The competition in the home electronics business is so fierce that strong ROI offers are a must. Circuit City, for example, runs commercials in which a father tells his young son that they can't buy the big screen TV because it might go on sale later for a lower price. At that point, the Circuit City announcer tells you that the store will honor the lowest price a consumer can find—at their store or any other—for 60 days after the purchase of the equipment. That generates trust and credibility, ensuring the buyer that he's going to get a good deal even if he finds a better price later. The effect is a profound risk-reversal in the mind of the consumer.

Why are they focusing on honoring any price 60 days later? Why not say that if they can find a better price on the spot they will honor it? Well, it's a brilliant understanding of their market. You, or someone you know, have probably purchased some electronics only to find it available for a better price later on. In fact, since the value of electronics quickly degrades as the latest and greatest models come out, this is an inevitability. This is a genius offer.

The only problem is, they aren't using it to create their identity. I would shorten it and use it as a pure identity builder over their currently very weak slogan of: "Just what I needed."

"48-HOUR PARTS SERVICE ANYWHERE IN THE WORLD— OR CATERPILLAR PAYS"

Caterpillar Tractor became a giant in the heavy equipment industry by promising its customers "48-hour parts service anywhere in the world—or Caterpillar pays." That's much like the Domino's Pizza offer in appeal—you're going to get what you need when you need it, or you're going to get it free.

I would imagine that people who purchase heavy equipment are quite conscious of the ROI they receive from their purchase. If this $200,000 machine is sitting there collecting dust, you certainly aren't earning an ROI. This Touchstone addresses that fear—and alleviates it—in a split second. Brilliant.

"TEN YEARS TROUBLE-FREE OPERATION"

Remember the Maytag repairman from the old TV commercials? The guy who sat around bored all day because no one ever needed a Maytag washer or dryer repaired? Well, that commercial was a spinoff of Maytag's original offer to their customers: "Ten years trouble-free operation." That's an impressive Touchstone. What do you want when you buy a washer or dryer? You want something that's going to get the job done, and you don't want to have to replace it for a very long time. Maytag addressed that need successfully.

"IF YOU'RE NOT SATISFIED FOR ANY REASON WE'LL TAKE IT BACK WITHOUT A RECEIPT—NO QUESTIONS ASKED"

Nordstrom's department stores do not compete on the basis of price. If you want to buy a suit, you'll find a cheaper one at other department stores. But Nordstrom's guarantees you that you'll be satisfied. They have had a long-standing publicized policy that anything you want to return will be taken back—no receipt slip necessary, no questions asked. That's a high ROI offer—for the money you spend, we're going to give you quality merchandise, and we'll even take it back if it's not exactly what you want. It keeps Nordstrom's successful despite the fact that it doesn't promise a bargain.

Obviously Nordstrom's isn't unique in this offer, but it demonstrates the effectiveness of such an approach on a large scale. The "without a receipt" portion also set them apart. It's a welcome change from the hell you get when normally trying to return something.

"THE 100 PERCENT SOLUTION"

Dave Liniger, the founder of RE/MAX real estate, was a marketing pioneer in his field. He turned his company into a billion-dollar business by creating the "100 percent solution." This Touchstone was directed not to the end consumer, but to his niche consumer: real estate agents.

You can keep 100 percent of your commissions, he said, and just pay RE/MAX a monthly fee for the office space, business cards, telephones, etc.

Liniger understood the significance of a loss leader. He was willing to give up money by forgoing a piece of his seller's commissions, knowing that he would draw scores of motivated people who would want to sell houses under the RE/MAX banner.

Because of this offer, he has thousands up thousands of reps paying him a monthly fee *and* building up his brand equity for him for free.

"BEFORE AND AFTER"

Offers don't have to be complicated or tricky. Most of the time, you want to show customers the value they will be receiving as simply and as directly as possible. Heck, you don't even need words (see the previous section on nonverbal communication).

Merle Norman Cosmetics is a prime example of simple nonverbal communication. When they decided to start advertising in magazines, they didn't use tricky catch phrase or fancy visuals. They simply showed a "before" and "after" picture of a woman, demonstrating how much more beautiful she was after applying Merle Norman products. This visual High ROI Offer caused Merle Norman sales to triple in the five years after that advertising campaign began.

Nonverbal communication can greatly enhance your overall presentation, but a verbal Touchstone will still improve your overall results. The Touchstone gives consumers a portable and easily transmittable way to spread your message for you. Try describing the Merle Norman be-fore and after to a friend. You'll probably need to find the picture and show it. Most of us don't carry such pictures around in our pocket's, but we do carry thousands of Touchstones around in our minds.

"FREE SAMPLES"

If you have a quality product that you know has the kind of high ROI that will attract and retain customers, then you should strongly consider a loss leader strategy to build your business. (Using your best judgment and keeping an eye on your ROI, of course.)

Debbie Fields, the founder of Mrs. Fields Cookies, thought she had a failure on her hands when she opened her first cookie store. By noon on her first day of business, nobody had come in to buy a single cookie. So, she filled a tray, went out onto the sidewalk and started giving cookies away for free. People immediately followed her into the store to buy more. That strategy has continued. With over 1,000 stores, every Mrs. Fields shop still invites customers to try a free cookie. The offer—we have so much faith you'll like our product, we'll give it to you for nothing because we know you'll come back to buy.

CHAPTER 11

Word of Mouth from Flaming Lips

The Irresistible Offer and Word of Mouth

Word of Mouth Marketing may be the most powerful marketing weapon in your arsenal.

Think about it—is there anything that would inspire you to make a purchase more than a trusted friend who is enthusiastic about the product?

Imagine you have some back pain. You complain about it to a friend, who says, "I had back pain for years, and nothing worked for me. I finally tried Egoscue Training, and it hasn't bothered me since."

What's the first two questions out of your mouth? Are you even asking any of the Big Four? No. . . . Amazingly, they've been bypassed.

Your natural reaction is:

1. What is that?

2. How do I get some?

Amazing, isn't it?

Why don't businesses focus all of their energy on Word of Mouth, then?

The problem is that its mechanisms are not well understood. Many will try to stimulate Word of Mouth, but the results are not reliably reproducible or measurable, so researchers give up in frustration.

Even if you understand the mechanisms of Word of Mouth so well that you can get people buzzing about you constantly, how can you be so sure that the message they are spreading is the right one?

That is, stories such as the Egoscue story above can't be manipulated. They happen spontaneously by dazzling your customers.

Can we put all of our eggs into the basket of hope that our customers will start spreading the word for us?

We could, but we might spend some sleepless nights wondering whether the hell it's working or not.

Does this mean that we shouldn't dazzle our customers? Of course not. This is what the High ROI Offer is all about. The better the ROI, the greater the Dazzle.

However, you can do a lot better than waiting for this kind of effect to kick in. It will kick in over time, but you can in fact speed up the process and improve your results.

The highest form of Word of Mouth is an active process stimulated by The Irresistible Offer.

To understand how and why, we need a little education about . . .

THE MECHANISMS OF WORD-OF-MOUTH MARKETING

Word of Mouth Marketing has really been around for as long as business itself.

I imagine even the first barter trades had people talking . . .

"Hey, where did you get that fly bison pelt, Samu?"

"Oh, I traded Zog some eggs for it. It's pretty pimp, right?"

"Word."

"It keeps me warm, and I don't have to clunk Ogda on the head for sex anymore."

"Trade? What's 'trade,' playah?"

One of the big buzz phrases of the last 10 years was "viral marketing." Numerous books have been written on the topic (many claiming they invented the term, but frankly no one knows who did), and they all describe various aspects of this new marketing fad.

Viral Marketing is really nothing more than another way of looking at good old Word of Mouth. Yeah, some Viral Marketing purists will take issue with this statement, but let's take a deeper look, and you'll really see they are one in the same (with the occasional exception of Delivery Mechanisms, which you'll learn about in a moment).

Language is a virus.
—William S. Burroughs

William S. Burroughs understood this. When he said that language is a virus, he displayed a deep understanding of Word of Mouth Mechanics.

A biological virus provides a truly apt metaphor for the mechanism of Word of Mouth.

HOW DOES A BIOLOGICAL VIRUS WORK?

A biological virus, by definition is simply a string of DNA or RNA surrounded by either a layer of lipid (fat) or protein.

The virus doesn't really exhibit any signs of "life" until it attaches itself to a host cell.

Once attached, it replaces part of the host cell's DNA with its own. The host stops what it was doing before and now has a new mission: make more viruses.

These fledgling viruses now float around until they attach to other cells and the process continues.

It's a pretty scary thought when you think about it. A virus uses your own body against you in order to spread itself.

In the case of a biological virus, the end result is pretty destructive as you know. However, the same mechanism can be used metaphorically for good.

Let's break it down.

In the simplest sense, a virus is composed of two things:

1. *A Program (a Set of Instructions).* The instructions are always, "Make more virii (spread the virus) and do something else." In the case of biological viruses the "something else" is usually something destructive. This program is always encoded into a strand of DNA or RNA, depending on the type of virus it is.

2. *A Delivery Mechanism.* How are these instructions passed around? Sometimes, they are delivered through the air (a cough or a sneeze). Sometimes, they are passed through simple skin-to-skin contact. Sometimes, it requires an actual transmission of bodily fluids (through the act of sex or intravenous needle sharing).

If a virus were missing any of these elements it wouldn't be anything spectacular. Put the two together and you have a self-replicating system par excellence.

LANGUAGE *IS* A VIRUS

Word of Mouth operates by essentially these same elements.

1. *A Program.* Remember, the program is simply a set of instructions: Spread the virus and do something else. That "something else" takes the form of an extra bit of information: either something good or bad to be communicated about your business. Oh yeah, that's right. Word of Mouth marketing is happening all the time whether you like it or not, whether the message is good or bad.

2. *A Delivery Mechanism.* In the form of Word of Mouth marketing, the Delivery Mechanism is, well, words from your mouth. However, it may be interesting to note that through our non-verbal communication we transmit Word of Mouth as well.

WORD OF MOUTH DELIVERY MECHANISMS

Information doesn't always spread by word of mouth per se, though. There are other mechanisms that can and should be employed, but let's take a look at the benefits of each.

Images

If you see a ring on someone's left ring finger, what do you automatically think?

That she's married, of course.

This is a classic form of information being spread through imagery.

Now, if you're paying attention, this information is communicated very quickly and efficiently through a single image. What happens, though, when you want to pass this information on to someone else?

Is this an ideal Delivery Mechanism for a Word of Mouth message?

Read on.

Sounds

Unfortunately, I can't play some example sounds for you, but maybe you can play them for yourself in your head.

Can you think of four notes you'd associate with Intel?

How about three sounds you'd associate with NBC?

How about the first three notes of every episode of The Simpsons?

Those sounds deliver a brand identity very efficiently, but they may not say much more. And what happens when you want to tell your friends about NBC? Do you hum their 3-note identity?

Words

The great thing about words is that they're infinitely portable.

If you want to tell someone that Mary is married, do you pop out a picture of her with a ring on her finger?

No, you say "she's married."

If you carried that picture with you, unless you were her husband, it might even be a little creepy.

If you want to talk about the company Intel, do you hum four tones? No, you say the word, "Intel."

Because of their portability, words are the fastest-spreading Delivery Mechanisms of all.

Memes

Memes are the most efficient form of communication around. By definition, they communicate entire ideas (even complex ones) in a single glance.

Images can be memes. (The cover of this book is a meme.)

Words are sometimes memes. ("I have a dream . . .")

And . . .

Great Touchstones are memes.

Read on . . .

With all of these choices, which Delivery Mechanism do you choose?

Further, how do you know that Word of Mouth is working in your favor?

Before that, let's learn a little more about how biological viruses spread for some clues.

VIRULENCE

Biological viruses, depending on their various attributes, are more or less virulent.

That is, they are more or less successful at spreading themselves and satisfying their programs.

Several things affect the virulence of a biological virus, and we can find interesting corollaries with Word of Mouth marketing.

Factors of Virulence for Biological Virii

This may sound a bit technical, but bear with me for a minute. Extending this metaphor even further will give us some incredibly powerful tools to make our Word of Mouth marketing unstoppably powerful.

Immunity of Host (Presence of Antibodies)

If you are exposed to a particular virus and you successfully fight it off, your body will have more success fighting it later on.

Sometimes, vaccines are given in order to increase your immunity in advance. This trains your body in how to detect a virus and in how to fight it if is infected.

These vaccinations can be so effective that they have all but eradicated many viral diseases that plagued humanity for centuries.

Host Strength or Weakness

If the host of a virus (the infected animal) is in a weakened state (due to age, injury, etc.), its overall ability to fight on a viral infection is lowered, even if it has a high degree of immunity to a particular infection. For example, you may have been given a flu vaccination, but if your overall strength is weakened your body's ability to produce antibodies in general is lower.

Replication Speed

If a virus is more efficient at replicating itself it will spread faster. Just think about it. If a single infected cell can produce more viruses, those viruses can then infect more cells, and thus produce more viruses, and so on . . .

Imagine, a tiny increase in replication speed can make a huge difference in the pace of an outbreak. Small changes in this rate can have an exponential effect.

Efficiency of Delivery

Even if a virus can replicate itself very quickly, it may not have much success spreading from person to person if the Delivery Mechanism is inefficient.

For example, if all someone has to do is stand in the way of someone coughing or sneezing to catch a virus, the delivery is extremely efficient.

If you need some form of physical contact with the carrier, the virus will spread at a much slower rate (because breathing is a much more frequent act than touching).

THE COPULATION RATE

Applying the biological model of viral growth to marketing, I was able to get some stunning results back in the early days of the Internet.

Back in 1995, I developed a formula that I applied to all of my Word of Mouth campaigns that allowed me to more effectively transmit my marketing viruses (although the phrase "viral marketing" hadn't even been invented back then, many of us were practicing it).

I measured the effectiveness of my campaigns by, for lack of a better term, "The Copulation Rate."

Copulation was a measure of the virulence of our campaigns. I didn't call it that until much later, but this rate was a tremendously powerful measurement to predict the success of your campaigns. It would allow you to put a number on your campaign and know instantly how well it would perform.

Copulation was measured in periods of time. That is, there was a 10-day Copulation Rate, a 30-Day Copulation Rate, and so on.

If your 10-Day Copulation Rate was 1.1, it meant that at the end of 10 days, on the average, one "Carrier" of your marketing "virus" would render approximately 1.1 new Carriers.

That is, one person who sees your message would render 1.1 new carries 10 days later. Or, 100 people who saw your message would spread the word to 110 new people and so on.

Theoretically, anything over a Copulation Rate of 1.0 was a good thing, since it meant that the pool of Carriers would progressively get larger and larger.

However, if the Copulation Rate was insignificant or over too long a period of time, any impact may not be seen during your lifetime.

For example, let's say that you have a 10-day Copulation Rate of 1.01. Assuming you start out with a pool of 10,000 carriers, let's see how quickly your campaign spreads:

A 10-Day Copulation Rate of 1.01

Day 0	10,000
Day 10	10,100
Day 20	10,201
Day 30	10,303
Day 40	10,406
Day 50	10,510
Day 60	10,615
Day 200	12,201

Not bad. At the end of 200 days your marketing message was seen by an additional 2,201 people without you having to lift a finger.

Pretty cool, right? It gets better.

Now, what if we were to increase that Copulation Rate by just 0.3 percent? Would the impact be significantly different?

Let's see.

A 10-Day Copulation Rate of 1.31

Day 0	10,000
Day 10	13,100
Day 20	17,161
Day 30	22,480
Day 40	29,449
Day 50	35,579
Day 60	50,539
Day 200	2,215,266

Not bad! By Day 10, a Copulation Rate of 1.31 outdid 1.01's Day 200 results.

And at the end of 200 days 10,000 people seeing your message turned in to 2,215,266 people seeing your message without your having to spend a dime on marketing.

Now, these numbers look great, and it's quite tough to get a Copulation Rate anywhere near 1.0 or more, but you see the potential.

So, how does one increase this Copulation Rate? How do you get such amazing results?

Easy, you increase your *Virulence.*

That is, you make your virus more and more contagious, so that it spreads at a more rapid rate.

FACTORS OF VIRULENCE FOR WORD-OF-MOUTH VIRUSES

The same factors that affect the spread of a biological virus can be applied metaphorically to the spread of Word of Mouth.

Immunity

Just as animals can build immunity to viruses through previous exposure, your target can become immune to marketing messages as well.

Immunity to a marketing message can be caused by many things.

Mistrust

If customers don't trust you, your products, your industry, your spokesman, they may be effectively inoculated against your marketing.

Maybe they've been burned by offers similar to yours. Maybe they've been burned by you. Maybe they just don't think that the products you sell work at all.

Overexposure

In general, repetition is a great thing in marketing. The more people hear your message, the more likely they are to respond to it. One piece of marketing lore that gets passed around from person to person claims that your prospects must hear your message exactly eight times before they will respond, but who knows if this is true? Some people may purchase your product with exactly one exposure (The Irresistible Offer makes this more likely), and some may never purchase. However, we do know that repetition helps, especially if you are trying to build a brand (and I hope you are).

"Overexposure" by definition means that your message has become old news, or stale news. It no longer captures the imagination or interest of your market.

This can happen when your approach stops being unique or relevant. For example, if pizza places everywhere started offering a "30 minutes or it's free" guarantee, the approach wouldn't have remained so effective for Domino's (or the copycats, for that matter).

Essentially, anything that has occurred before your contact with your prospects that predisposes them to be less receptive to your message will Inoculate them to your message and have a negative effect on Copulation.

Host Strength

A strong host is one that is by nature immune to a virus, regardless of previous exposure.

If the targets are weakened, they are more likely to be infected with, and thus pass on, the virus.

For example, if people are in a dire state of need for something, they are in a weakened state.

As cold and manipulative as it may sound, if you can imagine people with a medical problem, a pain, or an insecurity, they are weakened and thus more susceptible to a marketing message that addresses those weaknesses.

Throughout my life my body fat level has bounced up and down as I rollercoastered through various levels of fitness (as I write this I'm in excellent shape, I'm happy to say). During the times that I was overweight I've found myself responding to the most incredible and ridiculous offers for weight loss solutions. In a strengthened state, I would find myself laughing at the clumsy marketing of those very same offers.

Many of the Offer Intensifiers listed above will by definition weaken your prospects and thus make them more susceptible to your message.

Replication Speed

How actively are people buzzing about your product?

Do they bring it up only occasionally when it naturally fits into the conversation, or is it a topic of conversation itself?

The television show *Seinfeld* enjoyed tremendous success. One of the main causes of its success was its status as a water cooler show. That is, people around the office water cooler, when they were slacking off and not working, needed something to joke about. The previous week's episode of Seinfeld was a rather frequent discussion topic.

People who didn't know what the guys were talking about didn't want to look as though they weren't "in" next week, so they'd tune in to the next episode of *Seinfeld* to avoid looking like social lepers.

Because there was a new episode each week, and because each episode was full of little taglines to spread around, the speed of Replication was incredibly high.

Efficiency of Delivery

Remember how airborne viruses spread quickly and blood-born viruses spread slowly?

Words are the airborne Delivery Mechanism of Marketing Viruses. Words spread through the air, and even across electrons, at an incredible rate.

Want to test this out?

Okay, right now, I want you to inform the person next to you of the existence of a historical figure named Mother Teresa.

Wait!

Before you do it, choose the Delivery Mechanism.

You get to choose between:

A. A Picture of Mother Teresa

B. Just Saying the Words, "Mother Teresa"

"Hey, wait a minute. If I show them a picture of her isn't that just as fast if not faster?"

Maybe so, smarty pants, but let me ask you this.

Do you **have** a picture of Mother Teresa?

You don't, do you?

You do, however, have the ability to form those words with your mouth, and so will the next person, and the next person . . .

HOW TO MEASURE VIRULENCE

All this sounds great, but what if you want some measurable impact on your marketing?

Should you just try to positively affect all of the various Virulence Factors and let the chips fall where they may?

Well, you could, and you'd probably get some decent results if you're really good.

However, I don't know about you, but I don't like to rely on hope and luck.

"Hope, Lieutenant Joyner, is not a course of action." A battalion commander of mine used to always recite this popular Army saying every time he caught me using the word "hope."

Over time, I realized that I could either hope for things to go my way, or I could plan, measure, and get results.

On the Internet, I would measure various aspects of my "Viral Systems" in order to increase the copulation rate.

A Viral System is one that is devised specifically with high Virulence in mind.

We'd send people through the system with the intention of influencing them to send others through the system as well.

An example of perhaps the first Viral System on the Internet was a site of mine (now defunct) called "StartBlaze."

StartBlaze was one of the first "traffic exchange" systems on the Internet. A traffic exchange is a system that allows people to earn and exchange web site traffic (visitors) with other "web masters" or web site owners.

The fact that it was a traffic exchange system isn't what was really interesting, though. What was interesting was the systematic way it virally grew itself.

144

It worked so well that the site became the 36th most visited web site on the Internet just six weeks after its launch.

At the core of it, StartBlaze was really nothing more than extension of the same model I used to popularize e-books back in 1994.

Search Engine Tactics, the book generally credited as having popularized the use of e-books on the Internet was downloaded over 1,000,000 times by 1998, when I stopped counting.

Why?

Well, it was as virulent as the typhoid fever. In retrospect, the book was just an early and rudimentary form of a viral model I used to create a great many marketing campaigns on the Internet.

I discovered that this viral model could be applied to a great many things later on—not just overt viral marketing systems but almost anything.

In e-books, it's really simple. All you have to do is package the book into an electronic form that is easily distributable (Adobe PDF files work great these days—they are viewable by anyone) and put the following words on the cover page:

You may distribute this e-book freely, sell it, or include it as part of a package as long as it is left completely intact and unchanged and delivered via this PDF file.

Those words resulted in 1,000,000 downloads of one of my e-books and can turn yours into a force that simply can not be stopped.

Once you unleash this on the Internet, it can spread itself, and it may continue to do so for years and years.

A GENERAL MODEL OF WORD OF MOUTH

Word of Mouth can be divided into a number of various steps. We'll look at how it applies to marketing on the Internet, analyze each step in detail, and then learn how it can be applied metaphorically to almost any form of Word of Mouth marketing online or in the real world.

Let's take a look at how this works.

Everything I've described can happen within just a few minutes on the Internet. People could be at our site learning about one of our products, then within minutes they would be installing our software and telling others about it.

Again, this system worked so well that StartBlaze became the 36th most-visited site on the Internet at the time within six weeks of it's release. Search Engine Tactics was downloaded over 1,000,000 times. The same system, applied to many of our products over the years, resulted in millions and millions of dollars in sales.

A General Model of Word of Mouth

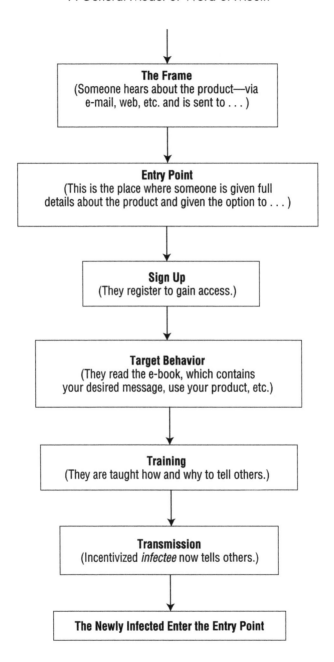

The Frame
(Someone hears about the product—via
e-mail, web, etc. and is sent to . . .)

Entry Point
(This is the place where someone is given full
details about the product and given the option to . . .)

Sign Up
(They register to gain access.)

Target Behavior
(They read the e-book, which contains
your desired message, use your product, etc.)

Training
(They are taught how and why to tell others.)

Transmission
(Incentivized *infectee* now tells others.)

The Newly Infected Enter the Entry Point

And my company was not by any means alone in this. ICQ, for example, had over 100,000,000 downloads of its instant messaging software before they were acquired by AOL. Their message was spread in very much the same manner, and they launched a brand-new category of software that is so large that there are four major competitors in the field that all have huge market share.

Napster, Hotmail, Incredimail—these companies and many others infected over 100,000,000 people each all through analogues of this same model.

How can you reproduce this?

Well, each step on the above diagram represents a critical Choke Point in the Viral System. There are literally thousands of things you could analyze when looking at any marketing process, but looking at these choke points allows you to focus on what can best affect Virulence and ultimately influence your Copulation Rate.

In fact, we found that if you made even tiny improvements to the conversion rates for each Choke Point, these improvements would add up and have a cumulative effect on our overall Copulation Rate.

Let's look at each Choke Point in detail, and the power of this model will become clear.

Keep in mind that not every Viral System will have distinct Choke Points as you see here. In the case of a viral e-book that is transmitted via a PDF file, it may simply be transmitted from friend to friend as an e-mail attachment. You can leave off the Sign Up step, and the frame and the entry point become blurred (the e-mail from their friend with the attachment serving as both).

Depending on your goals, variations of this model should be custom-tailored for your campaigns.

Leaving off the Sign Up step wouldn't be advisable if your desired goal is to collect a number of e-mail addresses.

If your goal is to simply create publicity for yourself, the Sign Up step isn't necessary. *Search Engine Tactics* didn't use the sign up step at first and relied solely on the rights statement to spread the book.

Simplifying steps can increase virulence, but every decision you make has a price and a consequence. Taking away the Sign Up will increase virulence, but will remove a benefit for you.

Got it?

Let's create a hypothetical case the illustrates the classic viral marketing model that works so well on the Internet:

a. *Entry Point:* You set up a web page offering a free e-book.

149

b. *Sign Up:* Your visitor must provide his information in order to be granted access to download it.

c. *Target Behavior:* Your visitor downloads and reads your e-book.

d. *Training:* You tell the reader of the e-book that he should pass it on to his friends so that they can also benefit from the information.

e. *Transmission:* The reader directs his friends to your URL where you offer the download of the book. The way he tells them about it and their opinion of him creates . . .

f. *The Frame:* The new infectee enters your Entry Point in a certain state of mind and we've gone full circle.

Again, every model will be different, but let's analyze this particular model in detail.

The Frame

This is the least visible, yet perhaps the most important step in the entire process.

The mental frame through which people view your Entry Point will, to a large degree, affect how they will react to it.

Do you remember that when we first talked about Word of Mouth we discussed how a recommendation from a friend can influence you to purchase a product, even if the marketing is otherwise bad?

This recommendation created a positive frame for you, through which you viewed the marketing of the product. The Frame was so important that it completely adjusted your perception.

Frames can have a positive or negative effect.

The Entry Point

This is the first exposure of a prospect to your formal marketing materials.

We need to assume the worst here and not rely on a positive frame to sell your customers. The study of advertising copy is generally focused on this step.

And, of course, this Entry Point can actually comprise several steps before the Sign Up.

That is, before your prospect is asked to actually respond, he may walk through a multistep Entry Point process.

For example, on the Internet someone may click on a Google Ad Word and then read a salesletter on your web site before being asked to respond.

Another case: Your customer may see your commercial on TV and then call in to talk to a salesman on the phone. Both steps of this Entry Point must function well before we can get anything of value from a customer.

Again, if you increase your conversion rate at this Choke Point (or any other one for that matter), you positively affect Copulation.

For example, if 2 percent of the people who view your Entry Point Sign Up that means that every 2 out of 100 people who get to this step will go further along.

Let's say that with this Entry Point conversion your Copulation rate is 1.01. If you boost your conversion at this step by 1 percent to 3 percent, does that mean that your Copulation rate will go up by 1 percent as well?

No!

It means that your Copulation rate will leap by *50 percent*. That is, 50 percent more people are going through your system altogether, so that you get a 50 percent increase in overall performance (Copulation) of the system.

Affecting conversion at earlier steps has exponentially greater impact on overall Copulation.

The Sign Up

Again, many Viral Systems bypass this step completely.

It is strongly advisable to require people to register your product (even your free ones) before they are granted access.

That way, if they abandoned the Viral System at any point you can always follow up with them and thus increase the conversion at the Choke Point where they dropped off.

Of course, this isn't always practical for all Viral Systems, but you should spend some serious time thinking about how you could incorporate this step into your Viral System in a seamless, nonthreatening, and unobtrusive way.

Target Behavior

This is the sole reason for the existence of your Viral System. That is, a Viral System without a Target Behavior is an aimless spread of information from one person to the next.

The Target Behavior for most businesses is a sale. In web-based Viral Marketing software systems, the Target Behavior is to have someone download and install a piece of software on their computer (the Google Desktop Search Engine, the Yahoo toolbar, MSN Instant Messenger, for example). In government propaganda campaigns, the Target is simply the spread of information itself—usually an idea or a piece of misinformation.

A great example of propaganda as target behavior can be found in the propaganda campaign carried out by France against the United States prior to the 2003 allied invasion of Iraq.

153

After the war ended, it came to light that agents of Saddam Hussein's government bribed French government officials with promises of oil contracts and corrupt UN Oil-for-Food Program kickbacks through misappropriation.

Before the war began and this motivation was known, the French perpetrated a great duping of the world and even of many American citizens. The French President Jacques Chirac delivered passionate speeches about how the United States was misguided and hasty in its decision to go to war with Iraq (even though France signed UN Resolution 1441 authorizing force against the Hussein government). Their propaganda campaign tugged at the heart strings and appealed to our desire for peace. On the surface, the French appeared to be the benevolent doves of peace (even though they wanted to influence the world to allow a murderous dictator to remain in power so they could benefit from corrupt oil contracts), and the United States appeared like a mad oil-hungry tyrant slavering to go to war.

This Viral System spread like crazy, and even after these facts have come to light, their propaganda has negatively affected the view of the United States in the world.

The Target Behavior was simply to adopt a pro-France and anti-United States attitude, and it worked both in the United States and abroad.

Training

The Training step educates your customer on two things:

1. Why they should spread the word (incentive).

2. How to do it.

In the StartBlaze system, our system was very deliberate:

1. Why?

Because you'll get more traffic to your web site. Lots of it.

2. How?

Here are several tools you can use to get the job done effectively (prewritten articles, product reviews, tell-a-friend tools, and so on).

We certainly made no bones about our intention of motivating people to spread the word. The Incentive and the How were all right there up front for anyone to see.

The effect was excellent, but frankly such overt and over-the-top approaches are not the best way to accomplish this. Deliberately bribing people to tell others about you certainly works, but people can smell the bribe on the breath of your promoters a mile away.

This is why many people in the Network Marketing industry end up in the NFL Club: No Friends Left. The network marketer is motivated to tell people about your product out of pure greed, and many times this will even inspire him to spread the word about crap.

There is just something unsavory about a bribe, and it taints the whole process.

In the case of StartBlaze, since it was a service for Internet marketers themselves, the target audience had a higher tolerance for the bribery. It helped that we were up front about the whole process and didn't waste anyone's time trying to be something we weren't.

The ultimate incentive is one that the transmitter of the virus isn't even aware of.

That is, if people find a bit of information funny, they may be motivated to pass this on to their friends. Indeed, some of the most viral things on the Internet are humor pieces.

But wait a minute, doesn't there have to be an incentive? How is a guy simply passing on a joke to his friend incentivized?

The incentive in this case is a bit subtler and 100 times more effective.

The incentive to you as the joke-spreader is this: You get to look funny and cool in front of your friends.

Anytime someone does almost anything, there is some incentive for doing so (be it an obvious one, a subtle one, or whatever).

The How, if not deliberately told, is intuitively known by your prospect: They open their mouths and spread the word—whatever that word is.

This Training process is occurring whether you like it or not. You may not be deliberately training your prospects the way I have in my more aggressive viral marketing campaigns, but you're still training them nonetheless.

Every interaction with your company, be it through your receptionist, your sales staff, or the cleanliness of your toilets, is providing potential Word of Mouth incentive.

If the toilets in your restaurant are spotless, someone's going to talk about it.

If someone finds a roach in their salad, I guarantee it will be talked about.

Just an hour before I wrote these very words, I received some Training from a company selling external laptop power supplies. Their batteries fried the computer of my business partner and simply didn't work for me. We tried to return the batteries and the company started putting us through a Kafkaesque hell of red tape and stonewalling.

We got the units back to them and FedEx called saying the company rejected the delivery because the return number was not written on the box.

They never told us to write the number on the box.

157

The FedEx agent very uncharacteristically informed me that "these guys are doing this all the time—they're a real nuisance." I'd never expect to hear words like that out of a FedEx employee's mouth. These guys must be *really* bad.

It didn't lower my opinion of FedEx one iota. It did, however, underscore my notion that this was a dead-beat company.

Did I just receive some Training? You bet! If I were a less-kind man I'd be telling you the name of the company now. Of course, to my friends and business associates, I'm sure the story will come up, and I'll gladly name the chumps who broke my friend's computer and then tried to skirt the refund for the defective merchandise.

My Incentive to tell you is the satisfaction I'll get in possibly preventing you from having your time and resources wasted with this Mickey Mouse outfit.

This company doesn't know it, but they Trained me very well.

On the other hand, if I had a great experience with them, I'd be telling people about how they helped make me more mobile, and they'd be getting even more business.

As a matter of fact, I ended up going to one of their competitors, batterygeek.net, and these guys gave me a smaller battery, with the same capacity, for about one-third the price, and I had no trouble whatsoever.

Their sales rep was even kind enough to give me some extra tips to make sure I didn't have any trouble.

Because of them, I now get about 12 hours of mobile battery life with my laptop (which is extremely important to me), and here I am writing about them in this book.

Transmission

Transmission for many affiliate marketing systems on the Internet is recorded by the use of tracking links assigned to each users.

If you don't know what affiliate marketing is, just take a look at Amazon.com—the company who pioneered this practice on the net. They offer a commission to you if you recommend a book to a friend. This is done by giving you these special tracking links and letting you distribute them as you see fit.

Amazon can then now, to a large degree, how many people each person in their system ended up subsequently telling.

New customers are also exposed to the opportunity to earn commissions on referrals, and the system continues.

As you can see, if you increase the Replication Speed (or Transmission Rate) at this step, more and more people will end up being churned through your Viral System.

You may not have the luxury of being able to measure every single time someone tells someone else about your business, but you sure can increase the Replication Speed.

More on this shortly . . .

Viral Systems on the Internet like Amazon's affiliate program may seem very deliberate and perhaps foreign to your marketing process, but this model can be applied metaphorically to the spread of almost any information.

You are probably using a Viral System of one form or another right now without even knowing it.

That is, every single customer who interacts with you goes through a process, you train him for good or for bad, and he passes this information on to others.

You are also involved in Viral Systems about yourself on a daily basis. If you stay at home all day, the Replication Speed of the (insert your name here) Virus is probably quite slow. However, if you're out in front of people all day long doing noteworthy things, your Replication Speed is significantly higher.

More on this later . . .

Virulence can therefore be measured by tracking and testing each of these Choke Points. Careful tweaking of what happens in each of these steps can render better and better results over time. And you may remember from our demonstration about tiny differences in Copulation, even the smallest changes will add up over time.

GENERAL TIPS ON VIRAL SYSTEMS

The following are just some general pieces of advice I have found that will increase the effectiveness of your Viral Systems.

In a second, we'll see how this all ties in to The Irresistible Offer in ways that will deliver some really dramatic impact.

Make it Easy

Any inconvenience, confusion, or obfuscation of your process will make people less likely to go through it.

Remember the Joe Vitale story of the Tacoma Chief I passed on to you? These guys didn't know how to make things easy for the consumer and definitely lost sales as a result.

People are bombarded with distractions all day long. If you add a tiny bit of confusion that delays the sale for even five seconds, that could be the difference between your prospects consummating the sale or allowing themselves to be distracted.

Imagine a guy at your web site. He's fired up and ready to buy. He's got his credit card out, but he just can't seem to figure out how to place an order on your site. While he's fumbling around scrolling up and down looking for the order button, his wife calls him to dinner.

161

Instead of saying "just a second, honey, let me just click send" he gives up and goes off to dinner, and most likely away from your site forever.

This can be applied analogously to almost any process. The easier it is, the more likely people are to do it.

Decrease Your Steps

One of the first things I show my consulting clients is the following graph.

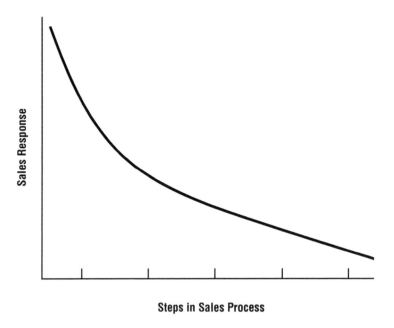

This graph is a gross generalization, but it gets the point across: the more steps you add to your sales process, the lower the response.

162

For example, there are companies with whom I have done business that have asked me to fax in a copy of my credit card and driver's license after placing a phone order.

This extra nuisance simply frustrated me as a buyer and prevented me from closing the deal with them.

Have you ever had this same experience?

I took this theory to the extreme by once simply posting a well-crafted order page to the web and directing my newsletter subscribers to it with an appropriate e-mail message.

The result?

We grossed over $100,000 in sales of a digital product in just two days.

There is not always a one-to-one correlation, but you get the idea. As few steps as needed to address the salient points to close the deal is best. If that takes 10 steps, it takes 10 steps. Obviously, if any step is crucial for response, you can't omit it just for the sake of lessening the steps in your process.

Be Excellent

People talk about things that are noteworthy. The thing most worthy of positive note is excellence—plain and simple.

Broaden Your Thinking on Incentive

Again, incentive can take many forms. Think creatively about what could possibly motivate your customer to spread the word about you, and you'll be surprised at what you can accomplish.

A classic tactic is to give your customers a meaningful gift certificate or discount voucher that they can pass on to their friends.

You don't feel bad giving out a gift certificate. Just don't give one to your wife for your anniversary, unless it's for a ring at Tiffany's.

Monetary Motivation is the Most Obvious, But Worst Incentive

Again, people can smell the bribe on those motivated through commissions to spread the word about your products.

Commission incentives can, and most certainly, do work but you shouldn't offer them as a band aid for the flaws of your product.

A good friend of mine recently launched a network marketing company and wanted to get me involved as the chief of marketing for the company.

After looking at his plans, I saw that his idea was an excellent one, but the product as it stood, I felt, was not one that people would consistently pay the asking price for. (They required a monthly subscription.)

I told him this, and he agreed. Instead of following my advice to continue to improve the product until people would gladly pay that price, and more, he decided to appeal to the greed of his promoters.

He said, "Yeah, people wouldn't pay that much for the product, but they'll stay in and continue to pay in order to continue earning commissions."

I thought it was a fatal mistake—and certainly one many, if not most, network marketing start-ups make.

I turned down the job and explained to him why. He said he'd take it under advisement, and I wished him the best of luck.

Today, the company is struggling. They created a tremendous amount of excitement about the product before the launch, but when the actual product and pricing plan were revealed, very few people upgraded to paying customers.

I never called him up to say, "I told you so," but I did e-mail him asking how things were going and offered my assistance gratis. He never wrote back and word is the process broke his morale. (I'm sure he'll bounce back.)

He was banking on greed alone to suffice as a big enough incentive—not just to spread the word, but also to keep on paying customers.

Obviously, it wasn't enough to do either.

There is no substitute for an ecstatic customer.

Study Other Viral Systems

Try to find out, from beginning to end, how this process works for other companies.

If you see an advertisement from a company you suspect may be very successful, every now and then you should become a customer of that company to see from the inside what they're doing.

Take notes every step of the way and continually apply what you've learned to your own company to improve your Copulation Rate.

THE IRRESISTIBLE OFFER IS THE ULTIMATE WORD-OF-MOUTH TOOL

The preceding pages about Word of Mouth were simply leading you up to the following four key realizations:

1. Words (be they spread through your mouth, e-mail, or print) are the most efficient, portable, and speedy Delivery Mechanism of all.

2. The best incentive for viral transmission is genuine enthusiasm.

3. You are involved in the creation and participation of Viral Systems all the time whether you like it or not.

4. You generally have very little control over what is said about you, but you can, in fact, influence this.

Point 4 is the real key: *You can stack the Word of Mouth deck in your favor.*

The Irresistible Offer, and I mean every bit of it, is preparing you to be a Word of Mouth master.

"Wait a minute . . . I thought The Irresistible Offer was about creating a High ROI Offer that becomes part of your identity. What the heck does it have to do with Word of Mouth?"

In a word: everything.

Let's break it down.

What are the three elements of The Irresistible Offer? HTB, remember?

1. A High ROI Offer
2. Believability
3. Touchstone

The High ROI Offer Generates Raving Fans

Remember how we said that there was no substitute for an ecstatic customer? How do you delight your customers? How do you make them your raving fans? You dazzle them. You give them more for their money than they ever would have expected.

People talk about that.

Some people will tell you that, to get people talking about you, all you have to do is stand out from the crowd. I disagree and for obvious reasons. If you stand out from the crowd and you suck, people will talk about you all right. They will talk about how silly you look *and* about how much you suck.

Gimmicky marketing doesn't generate raving fans. Excellence does.

And raving fans are contagious.

Raving fans have a high Replication Rate, and the efficiency of their Delivery is extremely high.

Remember that Immunity to your message will go down dramatically if the target hears about it from a friend.

Here's another way to destroy Immunity.

Believability Is the Immunity Killer

A virus can't catch hold if the host is Immune to it.

Remember: Your prospects can become immune to your marketing message, most commonly because of mistrust.

If you drench yourself in believability factors, as outlined earlier (go back and master this), the mistrust of your prospect will be deflated.

The Touchstone as the Ultimate Virus (the Ultimate Delivery Vehicle with the Ultimate Program)

Remember, a virus has two important aspects: a Program and a Delivery Mechanism.

To recap: The program says "replicate yourself" (at a rate determined by the Replication Speed) and "something else." That something else can be anything.

If your "something else" is something meaningful, there is more or less impact.

The Delivery Mechanism is one that more or less facilitates Virulence.

If we were to craft the Ultimate Virus, it would look like this:

1. Extremely fast replication speed

2. A delivery mechanism that floats like the wind

3. A program with impact

If a virus simply gives you a cold, the impact isn't that great. If it gives you anthrax, the impact is huge.

Marketing Viruses, of course, have these attributes as well.

A Touchstone is a quick, short memorable sentence that is delivered with the greatest of ease.

It is also delivered with great speed because if it's interesting, it gets people talking. If you're old enough to remember back when, I'll bet you've had some conversations about "30 minutes or it's free" and about the "12 CDs for 1 cent" Touchstones.

It is also the program with the greatest Impact.

And this is perhaps the most important point of all.

People are probably going to talk about you at some point. If you don't take matters into your own hands, this discussion could be good or bad.

If, however, you provide a short memetic device (your Touchstone) that conveys the ultimate message to those who hear it, you've succeeded in totally controlling the process.

Some Touchstones are so persistent that they remain around even after companies stop using them.

When you talked about Domino's, what was the one thing that always came up in a conversation?

"30 Minutes or It's Free."

When you wanted to order a pizza and you were in a hurry, was there ever a time when someone didn't suggest:

"30 Minutes or It's Free."

Have you ever sat around with a gathering of people and heard a story about someone who got a late free pizza from the guys who say . . .

"30 Minutes or It's Free."

Can you even think about Domino's now without thinking about . . .

"30 Minutes or It's Free."

This is the power of the Touchstone. Without this, Word of Mouth for Domino's could have gone in any direction. However, they absolutely captured and dominated our minds. They completely *owned* the Word of Mouth process.

Because this Touchstone was so persistent, it drowned out virtually every other bit of information you could associate with them.

And because this is an extremely well-crafted Touchstone, this information that is so thoroughly entrenched in your brain about Domino's is a risk-reversing, trust-building, curiosity-generating, word-of-mouth-stimulating, and otherwise sale-inducing nugget of pure gold.

If people are spreading information about you, wouldn't it be great if the information they spread could do all that?

WHY NOT OTHER DELIVERY VEHICLES?

At this point, I doubt you need to be sold on the power of the Touchstone. Just to put some nails in the coffin of pre-TIO marketing, let's just examine a few.

Why Not Images?

Images can convey a meaning with just a glance.

Without even having to say a word, you can show people an image, and they will instantly learn something.

If images are so efficient, why not use them instead of a Touchstone?

Well, you don't exactly carry the appropriate images around with you, do you?

It's like the difference between an airborne and a blood-borne virus. The virus that travels through the air does so much more efficiently at a much faster rate.

Wait a minute, you're right that people don't carry around images with marketing messages in their pockets, but they do *wear them. . . !*

Why Not a Brand?

We sure do wear images that convey marketing messages. Most of us do this every single day (on the clothes we wear and the accessories we carry).

We also drive them (your car), we play sports with them (balls and bats and such), we play them (guitars, pianos, and such).

Isn't that an infinitely better way of spreading your marketing message?

No one can deny that logo branding on portable items can have a tremendous positive impact on your business, but there are a few drawbacks that may not be immediately apparent.

Branding Takes Time

If you're a brand-new clothing company people won't recognize your brand right out of the gate. In fact, brand-conscious people will be skeptical of it until they have made an association with your brand that gives them the green light: "The cool kids are wearing this."

You can't simply flip the switch on a graphic brand identity. With a Touchstone, you have full control of the message from Moment One.

You Have Little Control over the Association

Brands mean different things to different people. I know some people who, after watching *Sex in the City*, associate Prada with the highest of fashion. I have another set of friends who have a completely different association.

Further, if your first exposure to a brand is someone wearing it that you find unattractive or uncool, then the logo will mean something very different to you. The association may not even be a subtle one. If a guy who stole your job from you wore Prada shoes, you'd probably have to watch a lot of *Sex in the City* episodes before the brand recaptured its cachet for you.

Again, with a Touchstone, the meaning is conveyed instantly in your choice of words. Nothing else will come through as loudly as that.

174

The Message Is Ambiguous

Sure, you may like Armani suits, but what does that brand really mean to you?

There is probably a long series of very subtle associations in your mind that compose your opinion of that brand, but could you verbalize them easily?

With a Touchstone, there is no Ambiguity.

Not Everyone Is in the Right Business

Some businesses easily lend themselves to the aggressive spread of a visual logo. Clothes, cars, companies with a fleet of delivery vehicles—all of these businesses have a great branding opportunity there.

What about your business?

Chances are, branding simply may not apply.

This doesn't mean I'm saying "don't brand." Not at all. What I'm saying is that The Irresistible Offer should become your brand identity.

If you have a logo, people should think of your Touchstone when they see it.

Case Study: A Touchstone Becomes a Brand

What does Lexus mean to you?

Well, it may mean a lot of things, but it probably isn't "cheap," and it probably isn't "Toyota."

Toyota, although it perhaps made some of the most reliably manufactured cars in the world, could never really get a foot-hold in the luxury car market. They didn't really have a lot of credibility after establishing themselves as a creator of reliable and economical cars.

So, what did Toyota do? In a stroke of genius, they created Lexus.

If you're driving a Lexus you're really driving a Toyota with some nice rims and comfortable features.

When Lexus came out of nowhere, they knew they had a tough job ahead of them. They wanted to be seen as a luxury brand, but also knew that it would be hard to be seen as one when there were so few luxury brands on the market, and all of them had been around for years.

So, they came up with a luxury-sounding name, hired a British actor for their commercials (in America we always seem to think anyone with a European accent is classier than we are), and developed a superb Touchstone: "Everything you'd want in a $30,000 luxury car, and a whole lot more."

It was brilliant. Lexus was a more affordable luxury brand, but with their Touchstone they removed the "affordable" stigma and firmly established themselves as a luxury brand.

> I still haven't become a Lexus convert, but kids younger than I who hadn't already established the luxury position in their minds with Mercedes were picking up on the Lexus brand like crazy. To them it simply *is* one of the luxury brands.

Why Not Any Old Meme?

If memes are the most efficient form of communication in the world, why not use any old meme to get the job done?

I know that a Touchstone is a meme, but isn't it the fact that it's a meme that's so important?

Actually not. You see, memes can mean absolutely anything at all. You can craft a meme to transmit virtually any message in the world.

If you haphazardly create a meme out of thin air to represent your company, you could be sending an unhelpful message or, God forbid, one that harms your image.

Memes can also be ambiguous in meaning. Some may require interpretation before you can grasp their full meaning.

Touchstones by definition transmit the right message. They do so instantly. And they do so without ambiguity.

177

If your purpose for reading this book was to improve the quality of marketing for your product or service, you should immediately go back to the beginning and read this book again.

This time be more proactive. Start taking notes and start planning exactly how you are going to apply these principles to your business.

Do you need to change your product? Do it!

Do you have all of the other pieces in place, but need a great Touchstone? Get to writing!

I can tell you right now without any doubt in my mind that 99 percent of the people who read this book will do absolutely nothing with this knowledge.

I once performed a demonstration at a seminar that illustrated this point.

I asked the audience (some 700 in attendance that day) to stand up if they had heard of the book *Think and Grow Rich* by Napoleon Hill.

Everyone in the room stood up. I asked then, for those who had not read the book to sit down. About 95 percent of the room remained standing.

Impressive! I applauded them for having read one of the most life-changing books in the world.

I then said, "If you don't believe that following the principles outlined in his book can make you rich and successful beyond your wildest dreams, I want you to sit down right now."

Everyone remained standing.

I said again, "Okay, you're telling me by standing up that you believe following Hill's principles in *Think and Grow Rich* will in fact give you all the success and money you could ever want?"

Everyone remained standing.

Then I gave them a little surprise. I said, "On page 38 of the trade paperback version of *Think and Grow Rich*, there is a passage called 'The Self Confidence Formula.' Hill says that you absolutely must recite this aloud to yourself, from memory, at least once a day if you want to have success with his book. You guys all believe his book will make you rich so surely one of you can stand up on the stage with me here and recite 'The Self Confidence Formula' from memory. If you don't think you can, please sit down."

Everyone sat down in silence.

I didn't even need to say anything. I sat there for a minute and let it sink in.

I then verbalized what we all knew. "Everyone here believes that following his book will make them rich and successful, but no one is actually following it. Why is that? Let's change that today. Let's start taking some action right now."

I'm sure that the vast majority of people who witnessed that demonstration are still in the same rut today that they were in two years ago.

A few of them may have changed and started taking real action in their lives, and I'll bet they are the most successful of the lot.

There are three words that I believe represent one of the most important keys to success:

Relentless Focused Action

You have to figure out what actions will lead you to your desired goal (that's the "focus"), and you must take those actions at a constant neverending pace ("relentlessly").

If you make the choice this moment to actually start applying this information, this will put you ahead of 99 percent of your peers.

Don't just set this book down and forget about it. Reread it and turn it into an action plan. Then execute that action plan relentlessly.

That, my friend, is the only way you will achieve any success of note in this life.

Mark Joyner

P.S. If your purpose in reading this book extends beyond the field of business, I want you to read Appendix A first.

Perhaps you want to sell yourself somehow.

Who wants to sell themselves?

Well, only people who want to be good students, husbands, salesmen, wives, parents, children, brothers, sisters, friends, and teachers.

If that isn't you, you don't need to read Appendix A.

APPENDIX **A**

Selling Yourself in Three Seconds or Less

U p to this point, the entire breadth of this book has been focused on The Irresistible Offer as it applies to the business of selling products and services.

Selling is something we're all involved in all the time, so it should stand to reason that the core theory of selling one thing applies to the selling of something else. Yes, every sale has its own nuances, but the same "Big Four Questions" must be answered, whether you're selling pizzas or selling yourself as a prospective friend.

Now, you may be thinking, "I would never sell myself! That's horrible! I think that's a very shallow way of looking at the world. I would sell a product, but selling myself? Never."

Perhaps, but let's ask a few questions and see if that's really true.

Have you ever applied for a job?

Have you ever applied to a school?

Have you ever tried to win the favor of a member of the opposite sex?

Have you ever tried to talk your friends into going to the movie of your choice?

Have you ever tried to convince someone you were right?

If you answered yes to any of those questions, then you're in the business of selling.

If we're going to do it, why not do it well?

If we believe that whatever it is we're selling is good for the other person, is there any harm in learning how to sell it a little better?

If you agree with that, then the following pages in this chapter are for you. If not, then there's no point in reading any further.

THE IRRESISTIBLE OFFER AS A METAPHOR

Sometimes the metaphorical application of a seemingly un-related theory can render some extremely useful insights.

A popular one is the metaphorical application of military tactics and strategy to business.

This approach is exactly why you'll see not only military leaders reading Sun Tzu's *Art of War*, but also Harvard MBAs.

Much of my last book, in fact, used military metaphor to illustrate my business theory.

An example. One of the most important military princi-pals is that of Surprise. That is, if you can surprise your op-ponent, you take away his ability to plan, and he must react in a befuddled state of mind.

Elaborate deceptions are often planned in order to gain the tactical advantage of surprise. In World War Two, for ex-ample, we sent General Patton to command an imaginary tank division in Dover to deceive the Germans into thinking that we'd attack France via the Pas de Calais, instead of in Normandy.

Military history is full of such deceptions.

This very same tactical principle can be applied to busi-ness as well. If you look at the history of the Microsoft and Apple conflict, you will find a great example of Surprise.

Microsoft began by creating the very first standardized Disk Operating System (DOS) for IBM personal computers. Well, they didn't actually create it, they bought it, but that's another story, which is truly worthy of study in its own right.

DOS was a command line operating system, which is very different from the graphical operating systems most of us are accustomed to today.

There was one competitor of note in the personal computer business called Apple. After a very skillful zero-cost acquisition of the mouse and Graphic User Interface (GUI) technology from Xerox, Apple thought that the IBM/Microsoft platform was no longer a threat.

Microsoft created software that would run on the Macintosh, and Apple felt they were in the position of power. Mac, after all, owned a GUI-based operating system and the computers on which it was run. Microsoft was just a software development firm who created, among other things, an inferior command line operating system to be run on IBM machines.

Bill Gates played his role very well as the little guy building software to be run on Macs. Steve Jobs, the CEO of Apple, never thought there would be a threat.

Secretly, however, Bill Gates was planning a major project: Microsoft Windows. This was a GUI-based operating system that would run on IBM machines.

Jobs didn't hear about this until it was too late. There is a famous meeting where, late one night, Jobs invited Gates to his office and asked him what he was up to.

Gates explained how it really wasn't a threat. He didn't intend for it to be anything that could possibly compete with the Mac. After all, Windows wasn't really an operating system—it was just a little novelty that would run on top of DOS.

And such was the deception that Jobs took hook line and sinker.

We all know the end result of this use of tactical Surprise: Bill Gates is the richest man in the world, and Apple is a computer with a relatively tiny niche market (artists, musicians, and people who want to feel special about themselves).

Now, no disrespect meant to Jobs. He is obviously a visionary, and the way he's kept Apple together through all of this (especially their plays with the iPod and iTunes) is truly impressive.

However, Gates simply out-maneuvered (another military principle) and Surprised him.

As you can see, the metaphorical application of military principles to business has rendered some stunning results. In this case, perhaps the most stunning result in history.

It works because world of business has many parallels to a battlefield.

The act of selling something in the commercial world has a great number of parallels to the use of influence in other realms as well.

That is, whether you're convincing someone to buy a product, watch a particular movie, or go home with you for sex, you are still convincing, and the same concepts apply on a metaphorical level.

Now, if you truly grasp these opening words of this chapter, you don't need the rest.

Simply applying The Irresistible Offer as a metaphor to any type of "selling" will render some really interesting results.

In fact, I highly recommend going back through the book and reading it in a different way. That is, how interesting would it be, if you read through the book once with the metaphor of dating in mind? What kind of insights would you find?

What if you read through it with the aim of learning to be a more influential parent to your children? How would you apply these ideas?

Here are some further clues you can use to make the translation easier.

THREE SECONDS

Just like a product or service, people are sizing you up in about three seconds as well.

Within the first three seconds of meeting you, people will make thousands of little judgements and observations that will culminate in some conclusions.

Do you look like a good potential friend?

Are you a kind person?

Could you be their lover?

Can they trust you?

Will you give them a good deal on that car?

If you present yourself in the proper way, you can either make it or blow it in those three seconds. Very few of us know how to take proper advantage of this little window of time. We let the chips fall where they may, and when they don't work out in our favor, we say, "It's not in our cards."

Yep, it is in the cards. Now, let's stack the deck.

THE BIG FOUR QUESTIONS

Do you remember the Big Four Questions? Let's imagine someone is meeting you for the first time and that they are running those same questions through their mind.

None of us would like to believe that we are so shallow as to judge the people we meet by these criteria, but let's suspend disbelief long enough, at least, to understand what I'm saying.

If you don't think you judge people this way, just consider for a moment that you are better than the shallow people who think this way and that you are learning how to deal with everyone else.

As for whether or not this applies to you, that's between you and your therapist.

Between you and Mark Joyner is how to better operate with those who think this way.

Okay, let's look at those Big Four:

What are you trying to sell me?

How much?

What's in it for me?

Why should I believe you?

Do you think those same questions apply? Let's take a look and see.

What Are You Trying to Sell Me?

Everyone has a list of criteria from which they operate. Unconsciously, people know this, and they are looking out for your game.

Some people are up front about what they want from a relationship. Sometimes people come to you feigning one thing ("All I want is to be your friend") and then you learn later that they really wanted something else ("Hey, can you introduce me to your sister?").

If you are up front about what you want out of your relationships you don't waste any time trying to be something you're not.

If you're a salesman and you're up front about your product, you'll quickly sort through prospects who aren't right for what you're selling and find the ones who are.

If, when you're out on the town, what you really want is girls for casual sex and you pretend like you're looking for a wife, you're going to have to weave an elaborate deception and waste a lot of time to get what you want—and at what cost?

If, on the other hand, you were up front about what you wanted, you'd sort through the ladies looking for husbands and identify the ones looking for the same thing as you.

How many hours of your life have you wasted trying to pretend that you're selling something you're not?

Deceiving people may make the first sale, but you certainly won't ever sell that Second Glass. If you did, it would be a miserable Second Glass for both you and your customer.

How Much?

You may not be asking for money in return for whatever it is you're selling, but there is always a cost.

As an author, people come to me all the time pretending they want something from my relationship that they don't.

For example, one "NLP (Neuro Linguistic Programming) Expert" once came to me using all sorts of poorly crafted and clumsy language patterns to convince me that he wanted to help me promote my book.

Over the course of a long painful conversation where I tried to figure out what he wanted and he kept evading the question, it became painfully obvious that he had no intention of promoting my book at all, but really wanted me to promote one of his products on my list of subscribers.

The cost of even talking to him was a whole lot of my time. The cost of the deal would have been high for me with absolutely nothing in return.

Maybe you are attracted to a beautiful woman who on the surface is everything you want. She seems to have a great heart, a bubbly way that makes you smile, she strokes your ego.

Then, as you learn more about her, you discover that she has some deep emotional baggage that is going to cause you a lot of pain and suffering over time. You discover later that she's not really what she seems at all and that you've wasted a whole lot of your time.

192

The Offer Is the Antidote to Shady Persuasion

If you always analyze things in terms of an offer, you will prevent yourself from getting burned every time.

Some people try to trick you into unfair deals with all sorts of clever language patterns and persuasion tactics.

If you simply look at any offer in terms of quid pro quo, you can see through this every time. A shady dealer will not be up front about what you get in return or what he intends to do. He'll try to get you to put your confidence in him and insinuate that you should just trust him. If you question him, he'll usually start to get offended.

When it comes time to collect on the insinuated return, he might say something like, "Oh, you misunderstood. I never promised that."

And on the surface of it, he's right. He never promised. You didn't ask for a clear offer, so it's really your fault for getting suckered in a way. It doesn't make the person any less of a scum bag for trying to take you, but it's your responsibility to defend yourself.

I always ask people one of two questions, or both:

"What is this deal exactly?"

"What is it you're offering?"

If you don't get a clear offer, don't walk away—run!

(Continued)

Sometimes people who don't have clear offers aren't all bad—they're just confused—and the impact they have on your business will be just as bad.

Find out what someone is offering, and if it is not a deal that meets the following criteria, don't take it:

1. *It must be a fair quid pro quo, or a win/win.* Sometimes, people are tempted to take deals that are onesided. If you ever enter into a deal where you benefit and the other party doesn't, you may think you're benefiting, but you're really not. One of two things will happen. Either your partners will feel sore about it and slander you six ways from Sunday, or they will feel sore about it and come back to you with a sense of entitlement. And they won't want something fair in return—they'll want more because their feelings are hurt.

2. *It must serve your objectives.* I used to feel obligated to take deals out of friendship or out of fear of hurting the other party's feelings. I'd always regret that move and I'd either end up backing out or being so bogged down with excess work that I didn't perform very well.

There is absolutely nothing wrong with turning down deals. If the other people persist or are angry, that's their problem. You're not their psychologist. If what someone is offering you is a fair deal, but it does not further your overall life purpose or goals, it's not a fair deal at all—it's just a waste of your time.

If you're happy doing favors that's something else, but remember not even favors are free. You'll probably expect something in return as well. Now, if you don't know what your overall objectives or goals are, you'd better sit down and figure that out fast. You're going to get taken time and time again if you don't know what you want out of life—in business, in friendships, everything.

3. Your gut must tell you it is the right move. You know, I don't really have a rational explanation for this rule. If you asked me to try, it would surely sound like a bunch of superstitious nonsense. However, I can tell you, without reservation or exception, that every time I've failed to listen to my gut it's gotten me into trouble.

Many of the genuine business experts I've spoken to over the years will tell you the same thing. Secretly, many of us are placing more value on intuition than we'd care to admit publicly. Learn to tune in to your gut and follow what it is telling you. Just let go and give this a try some time. Try it with something small, and as you gain more faith in your own intuition, you can trust it more and more with bigger things.

That's the cost, my friend.

If you can lower the cost of dealing with you by not re-quiring so much emotional energy, perhaps that will make your offer more irresistible?

"What's in It for Me?"

How are you going to benefit someone as a friend or a lover?

Okay, so you want to be someone's lover. Ask yourself, if someone on the street made this offer to you, what would you say to yourself?

You'd analyze and evaluate in terms of how you'd bene-fit. Okay, so maybe you don't judge people on their looks or by other such shallow yardsticks. Maybe you prefer peo-ple who are genuine, honest, and stable. Well, guess what? That's how you benefit. That's what's in it for you. If they meet those criteria, you'll be more likely to accept the offer. If they don't, you'll reject them because there's nothing in it for you.

"Why Should I Believe You?"

Okay, so you are offering something they want. The cost does not appear to be too high. What's in it for you seems to be something wonderful.

Then you get this sinking feeling in your stomach that maybe this offer isn't exactly what it seems.

You may be giving off some credibility-defeating signals that will prevent you from closing many deals in your life.

THE TOUCHSTONE (THE ME MEME)

"Hi, my name is Mark Joyner, and I'll have sex with you in 30 minutes or less or it's free."

Okay, maybe that wouldn't work.

The Touchstone for selling yourself takes on a slightly different form.

If you're selling yourself as a consultant, a verbal Touchstone will work as it would for any other product. If you are the product in the professional world, you can be a little more overt about your offer, and you can get away with it.

Outside of the business world, your approach needs to be a bit less direct. Maybe it's the inherent hypocrisy of the world. Maybe it's the arbitrary rules society has thrust upon us. For whatever reason, we need to communicate our offers a little more subtly when it comes to personal interaction.

You can be up front about the nature of your offer, but you probably won't get away with throwing it in someone's face. (Depending on the context, of course.)

Your Touchstone is a mimetic one. When people first meet you, various pieces of information come together to form a mimetic expression of one idea: *you.*

When I first meet someone I'm aware that my appearance, my posture, my facial expression, my grooming, my clothes, the first words out of my mouth. All of these things come together to form the Mark Joyner meme.

Depending on what you want, your Me Meme may or may not serve your purpose. If your intention is to find a hot date, you may want to adjust your Me Meme from the "trust me as your salesman" Me Meme.

How you adjust these elements is a totally subjective thing. To me, the following elements make up the MJ Meme under ideal conditions:

Clean, pressed, fashionable clothes

If I'm out on the town, throw in "slightly funky." If I'm trying to make business contacts, replace that with "professional." Other Me Meme elements include

Impeccable grooming

Friendly smile

Confident posture

Outgoing and kind nature

My spirit shining through

First words: Something disarming and friendly

Over time, I've learned that is what I want to express to the world.

Some people may read those words and want to vomit, and that's okay. Cynical and sarcastic people may not like guys like me, and that's cool. My Touchstone (the MJ Meme) will sort right through them. I don't want to be around them, and they don't want to be around me. No worries.

Guess what? Less time wasted. More signal—less noise.

I don't care what your Touchstone is, but you would be wise to ask yourself: Is it serving my purpose?

If your Touchstone tells people you are a stuck-up snob who only cares about appearance, and secretly you want to meet some very down-to-earth genuine people, then perhaps it's not serving your purpose as well as it could.

On the flipside of this, I have trained myself to be careful about how I allow people's Touchstones to affect my judgment of them. The image most people are projecting to the world is not a genuine one. Thank Hollywood for twisting our brains and injecting values in us that are not our own.

At the same time, regardless of their intentions, the Touchstone they have chosen is theirs, and it will give some clues about what they're all about.

199

That is, no matter what the reason, if someone always looks like a train wreck, it might be indicative of greater levels of disorder in his life.

Then again, the best-groomed guy in the world could end up being like a train wreck through *your* life!

THE HIGH-ROI OFFER

If you have read the last few pages that talked about how the Big Four Questions play out in relation to selling yourself, you already know what I'm about to say.

If what you're offering people renders a great return for a fair cost, it will be easy to buy what you're selling.

Is this a shallow way of looking at things?

Isn't it manipulative to look at life in terms of selling yourself?

Not really. If anything, looking at life this way will allow you to operate under a much higher level of integrity than the alternatives.

BELIEVABILITY

Again, your offer must have some believability to it.

If what you're offering is a deal that is too good to be true ("Hey baby, I just want to be your friend. I respect that you have a boyfriend. Honest!"), people will immediately treat you with skepticism.

Your mannerisms, your appearance—all of those elements that make up your Me Meme—they all play a card in someone's evaluation of your trustworthiness.

I once visited a company I was considering promoting a few years ago. Everything they did over the course of two days was perfect.

The morning of my departure, the company president picked me up to drive me out to the airport.

He said one single thing to me that threw the whole deal out the window. He offered me a few percentage points of the company for $50,000.

Now, this immediately told me several things:

1. The company was not as financially fit as I thought.
2. Perhaps they weren't upfront with me about what they really wanted from our relationship.

One little tiny believability killer threw the whole deal.

Everything you say and do can have the same effect in your social interactions as well.

THE GREAT FORMULA

Remember the elements of The Great Formula?

The Irresistible Offer

A Thirsty Crowd

A Second Glass

If you follow the above rules and truly have The Irresistible Offer, your Second Glass is a done deal. Why wouldn't people want what you're offering again and again?

Everywhere you go, there are certain likely assumptions you can make about the people who are there. For example, if you want to meet people whom you would like to support a charitable project you have in mind, would you go to the beach to find them?

If you're trying to meet a nice woman who might be a good mother to your children, would you go to a strip bar?

Do you get the idea? Figure out where your Thirsty Crowd is hiding, and spend your time there.

You can further sort through your prospects by being as upfront about your offer that social conventions will allow.

Now, this may not apply when your customer is predefined for you. Can you apply this to your children or your friends? Of course not, but you can get them to come back for a Second Glass when what you give in that relationship truly serves both of your interests.

The problem is that we're so tuned in to our own radio station so much that sometimes we are totally out of synch with even what those we love want in life.

WORD OF MOUTH

If people are getting the goods from you, whatever it is that you're selling, word is bound to spread.

Now, the dynamic is a little different because there is no way people can spread your Me Meme around for you, but they can spread one piece of very portable information: your name.

Does this matter?

If your reputation precedes you, do you think that will help matters?

Perhaps this little sidebar will make that clearer.

I suspect that the Frame is so powerful because it is very subtle and almost unconscious. It is also because we have associated the preframe information with something in our minds that we have already allowed to enter unfiltered. That is, if we develop trust with someone, information we get from them bypasses our mental filter and penetrates deep into the core of our beliefs.

If you don't yet understand the power of this, I highly recommend paying close attention to your own mind. See how your beliefs affect your opinions. What is your political

The Greatest Persuasion Secret in the World

If you understand this one secret, you can dispense with just about every other book on the topic of persuasion and still get some great results in your life.

Keep in mind that I have been a lifelong student of persuasion, have written respected books on the topic, and have seen how persuasion plays out in many various contexts and battlefields.

I can tell you, without question, that the following concept is the Holy Trump Card of all persuasion principles: The Frame.

The Frame is not your message—it's the message that precedes your message.

Huh? Stay with me . . .

Imagine for a moment that you are looking at a piece of art in a museum. What kind of assumptions would you make about it?

The underlying presupposition is that the art is worthy of being in a museum. It must be good.

What if you saw the same piece of art being peddled by a street artist? Do you think your perception of it would be different?

I mean, if he's any good, what is he doing selling art on the street, right?

I heard possibly one of the best explanations of this principle from the most unlikely place once: a chick flick entitled *Never Been Kissed.*

Drew Barrymore played an undercover reporter who was sent back to high school to write about what life is like for teenagers these days.

Barrymore's character was a real dork in high school, and she discovered that she was still just as much of a dork when she went back undercover.

Her brother (played by David Arquette), an otherwise unsuccessful guy who was a popular baseball jock in high school, decided to enroll in the school and help her out.

He quickly became the most popular kid in school and began his campaign to save his sister's self-esteem.

He told everyone that she used to be his girlfriend and that she dumped him. He spoke reverently about how great she was and within the matter of a day, she was quickly accepted as one of the cool kids.

He summed this up with one line: "Josey, if you want to be cool, all you have to do is get one other cool kid to like you."

When the other cool kid likes you, this preframes everyone else's opinion of you.

Their contention was that even the cool kids were absolutely terrified of everyone finding out their secret: that they are just as dorky as you. The other cool kids give something acceptance and the green light: It's safe to like it now without being found out.

I think it's a pretty valid analysis.

affiliation? When you hear a representative of the other side talking, how do you tend to respond?

Also, pay attention to how the preframe info affects the opinion of others.

For a fun experiment some time, try this with the wing man of your choice.

1. Go to an area far away from where you live.

2. Go to a bar or a club with your wing man five minutes behind you and strike up a conversation with someone.

3. Half the time, before your friend enters the bar, tell the person to whom you're talking that your friend is a famous movie producer. The other half of the time, tell them that he just got out of prison for assault.

4. See how that affects how they react to him.

Wait a minute. Maybe you already know how this is going to play out without going through the trouble.

Do you now see the power of the Frame?

With the proper preframe, do you really think you'll need any other persuasion tricks to attain your objective?

This is why Word of Mouth is the most powerful form of marketing in the world.

Warning: some people who first learn this principle use it to deceive people. When people find out you were lying, not only will you lose your Second Glass, but Word of Mouth will start to have the exact opposite effect on your life.

A Note to Salesmen

f you work as a salesman in any organization, you may feel helpless if you are selling a product that is not backed by The Irresistible Offer.

Yes, salesmen who are blessed with that luxury are going to have a much easier time of things. However, if are not one of them, do not despair. There are still many ways you can apply these ideas that will boost your results dramatically.

Let the following considerations be your guide.

1. Remember the first sale you make is yourself.

Before your customers will buy a product from you, they need to be sold on *you* as a salesman.

Go back and read the Chapter: "Selling Yourself in Three Seconds or Less."

2. What is your Touchstone (your Me Meme)?

Is it one that is conducive of the sale or not?

I once called a hair-replacement company (yeah, I'm going bald—deal with it) and was asked to come in for a consultation.

Generally, companies like this will not tell you too much on the phone, but will rope you in to the office so you can be influenced by their slick sales pitch.

I went in expecting a very polished and professional piece of influence.

What I saw instead totally surprised me. I was greeted by a salesman with the most ridiculous looking rug of a hairpiece on his head. The deal was pretty much killed in that first instant, but I thought I'd stick around and give it a chance. Hey, maybe this was a bad example, and yeah going bald really sucks.

If you could imagine a used-car salesman trying to talk nicely to a five-year-old with a learning disability, that would be a little less insulting than the way this guy talked to me.

I hope that's not what you want to project to your prospects. I hope that you want to project honesty and respect, and I hope that you really mean it. If you don't, do yourself and the world a favor and get out of sales.

What to Do If You're Selling a Product Marketed by The Irresistible Offer

If you're this lucky, feel blessed. Your job of selling is going to be very easy.

In fact, you probably won't talk to many prospects who aren't ready to go.

Just answer questions honestly, be helpful, honestly ask yourself if your product will serve this customer, and communicate that fact clearly.

If your product is wrong for your prospects, quickly sort through them, send them to someone who *can* help (that will create some great Word of Mouth, believe me), and move on to the next prospect.

Yes, it's really that simple.

What to Do If You're Selling a Product without The Irresistible Offer

First, give a copy of this book to your Director of Marketing and your CEO. You probably won't see the impact right away, but maybe a year from now you will. Remember, it will take time for them to incorporate this into their marketing (more or less time depending on the level of bureaucracy).

You'll thank yourself for an easier job and more commissions later.

Meanwhile, remember to sell yourself first.

Next, see if you can create The Irresistible Offer on your own. Go through and create one for your product, and start using it on your prospects (if your organization is flexible enough to let you do what you want).

Can you create some added benefit that will increase the ROI of your offer?

Maybe as your sales stats increase, they will lead to a promotion and a raise. Then again, maybe the increase in commissions alone will be enough.

# GLOSSARY

Believability   One of the three elements of The Irresistible Offer. Without Believability, you could offer the world, and no one would take it from you.

Big Four Questions, The   In an Unspoken Inner Dialogue, your consumer asks himself four questions before making any purchase. These questions must be answered by your marketing, or the sale will not be closed.

"What are you offering?"

"How much?" (what is the "cost," be it monetary or otherwise)

"What's in it for me?"

"Why should I believe you?"

Copulation Rate   The rate at which a Viral Marketing System spawns new users of the system. A ten-day Copulation Rate of 1.01 means that any user of your system spawns 1.01 new users every 10 days. Rates can be calculated over any desired period of time.

Core Imperative of Business, The   There is one thing, and one thing only, that you must do to be in business: "Make an offer." If you are not offering your customer some form of quid pro quo, you are not in business.

Great Formula, The The way to long-lasting business success. Present The Irresistible Offer to a Thirsty Crowd, and then sell them a Second Glass. In other words, you take your TIO marketing to your warm market—those who are eager for your products. Then, once you have dazzled them, you leverage that relationship and make more money by selling them additional products and services they need.

High ROI Offer An offer that presents to the consumer a high Return on Investment. If you give the consumer more than his money's worth, that is a High ROI Offer. If you give him less, it is a Negative ROI Offer.

The Irresistible Offer The Irresistible Offer is an *identity-building offer central to a product, service, or company* where the believable return on investment is communicated so clearly and efficiently that it's immediately apparent you'd have to be a fool to pass it up.

Meme A unit of information that replicates itself from one mind to another via various transmission mechanisms (words, pictures, behavior, etc.). The term was coined by Richard Dawkins in his book *The Selfish Gene.*

Offer Intensifiers Elements that can intensify the impact of your offer. Offer Intensifiers can be used without TIO to increase sales, but this is not advised. They are only meant to enhance the impact of TIO—not replace it.

Risk Reversal One of the most powerful Offer Intensifiers. Consumers see any purchase as a risk (as illustrated by The Big Four Questions). Demonstrating that the consumer is not taking on any risk can greatly impact sales by alleviating worry. This can be accomplished via many means (see the chapter on Offer Intensifiers).

Second Glass   Any time you sell a product or service to already existing customers, you are selling them a Second Glass.

Special Offers   To be distinguished from The Irresistible Offer: TIO is an identity building offer, Special Offers are short-term deals to drum up a short-term increase in sales.

Thirsty Crowd   Your warm market. These are the people who are eager for your products and services without having to be told they need them.

Three Second Rule, The   Anyone seeing your initial advertising will give it about three seconds—in those three seconds they decide whether or not your offer is for them. Your Touchstone must convince them within that time frame.

Touchstone   One of the three elements of The Irresistible Offer. It communicates the essence of your offer in less than three seconds.

Unspoken Inner Dialogue   The internal dialogue we say to ourselves unconsciously that dictates many of our actions.

Viral Marketing   An analogue of Word of Mouth Marketing that uses technology to transmit your marketing message as a biological virus transmits itself from one host to the next.

Word-of-Mouth Marketing   The sometimes passive transmission of your marketing message from one person to the next simply through personal verbal referral.

INDEX

Action plan, developing, 178–180
Amazon.com, 159
Anacin, 31–32
Apple Computer, 186–187
Army, Touchstone of, 114–115
Art of marketing, 100
Awards, 50

Batterygeek.net, 158–159
Believability:
    credibility and, 49–52
    magic formulas for, 47–48
    proof and, 48–49
    RackSpace Managed Hosting
      and, 118
    selling self and, 200–201
    Word of Mouth marketing and,
      169
Benefit, 27, 29
Big Four Questions, 9–14,
    189–192, 196–197
"Biggest Sale Ever," 25
Birthday cards, 72–73
Boutique marketing, 110
Bragging rights, statement of, 27
Brand value, 94–96, 173–176
Brevity of Touchstone, 42
Bribery, 155–156
Business, as chosen metaphor for
    book, 16
Buyer, logic and emotion of, 13–14
Buyer insecurity, 11–12

Caterpillar Tractor, 121
Choke Points, 148–150, 160
Churchill, Winston, 39
Cialdini, Robert, *Influence*, 91

Circuit City, 120–121
Clarity of Touchstone, 41
CNN, 117
Coercion, marketing through, 18
Columbia House Records, 43–45
Commission incentives, 164–166
Communication, nonverbal, 46,
    123–124
Consulting services, 69
Continuity products, 67–68
Continuums:
    commonness of solution for
      problem, 106
    comparisons to competition,
      108–110
    demonstrable return on
      investment, 107
    emotionality of offer, 107–108
    genuineness of need, 104–106
    obviousness of need, 102–103
    overview of, 101–102
    timeliness of offer, 108
Contrast in pricing, 91–92
Contrived urgency, 78–79
Copulation Rate, 135–138
Core Imperative of Business, 5–7
Coupons, 92–93
Creation process, steps for, 52,
    56
Credibility, 49–52
Cross-sell, 65–66
Customers:
    ecstatic, 166, 168
    helping, 66
    high profile, 50
    sales process and, 53
    tricking, 39

De Beers, 105
Deceit, 206
Decreasing steps in sales process, 162–163
Delivery mechanisms of Word of Mouth marketing:
  branding, 173–175
  images, 130–131, 172–173
  memes, 132–133, 177–178
  sounds, 131
  words, 132
Diamond rings, need for, 105–106
Discounts, 92–93
Domino's Pizza, 22–23
  guarantee by, 20–21
  history of, 19–20
  quality of, 21–22
  return on investment and, 38–39
  Touchstone of, 43, 171–172

Ease, 88–89, 161–162
E-books, 145–146
Education, selling, 69
Efficiency of delivery mechanism, 135, 142–143
Elements of Irresistible Offer:
  Believability, 47–52
  high ROI, 36–39
  overview of, 35–36
  Touchstone, 39–46
Endorsements, 49–50
Entry Point, 151–152
Excellence, 163

Fact, statement of, 27
Factual proof, 48–49
Federal Express, 45–46
Fields, Debbie, 124
Follow-up, 66–67
Fox News, 116–117
Frame, 150–151, 204–205
Freebie marketing tips, 75
Free samples, 124
French propaganda campaign, 153–154

Gates, Bill, 186–187
Genuine urgency, 78
Great Formula:
  Create Irresistible Offer, 56
  Present to Thirsty Crowd, 56–57, 60
  selling self and, 202–203
  Sell Second Glass, 60, 63–64
  steps in, 55–56
GSD&M (advertising agency), 30
Gursich, Steve, 30
Guthy-Renker infomercial marketer, 67–68

Halbert, Gary, 85
Headline, testing, 61–62
High ROI offer:
  logical additions and, 71
  overview of, 36–39
  selling self and, 200
  Word of Mouth marketing and, 38–39, 97, 168
Host strength or weakness, 134, 140–141

ICQ, 148
Identity-building offer, 15–17
Images, 130–131, 172–173
Immediacy of Touchstone, 42
Immunity of host, 134, 139–140, 169
Impatience of consumers, 1–2
Implying something, 116
Incentives, 156, 164–166
Influence (Cialdini), 91
Information, transmission of, 46
Insurance, selling, 70
Intensifiers:
  added value, 79–80
  brand value and positioning, 94–96
  ease, 88–89
  overview of, 77–78
  pricing tricks, 89–93
  recommendations, 97
  risk reversal, 80–86
  scarcity, 86–87

Index

uniqueness, 93–94
urgency, 78–79
Intuition, 195
Irresistible Offer, 15
    emotion and, 107
    vs. Special Offer, 26

Jobs, Steve, 186–187

Keeping door open, 71–75
Kennedy, Ted, 13

Lexus, 176–177
Liniger, Dave, 122
Logic, appealing to, 50–51
Loss Leader technique, 63, 64,
    82–83

Magic of marketing, 100
Magic window, 3–4
Marketing, *see also* Word of Mouth
    marketing
    art of, 100
    magic of, 100
    science of, 99–100
    through coercion, 18
Master, definition of, 11
Maytag, 121
McDonald's, 87
Memes, 132–133, 177–178,
    197–200
Merle Norman Cosmetics, 123–124
Microsoft, 185–187
Military metaphor, 185–188
MindControlMarketing.com
    (Joyner), 18
Monaghan, Tom, 19–21
Monetary incentives, 164–166
Money-back guarantee, 80–82
Morphogenic fields, 100
Mrs. Fields Cookies, 124

Need:
    genuineness of, 104–106
    obviousness of, 102–103
Network marketers, 155–156,
    164–165

Never Been Kissed (movie),
    204–205
"New and Improved," 25
Newsletters, 73–74
Nonverbal communication, 46,
    123–124
Nordstrom's, 122

Offer:
    as Core Imperative of Business,
        5–7
    identity-building, 15–17
Offer Intensifiers, *see* Intensifiers
One-Click-Upsell, 58
Order form, testing, 61–62
Overexposure, 139–140

Package deals, 69–70
Paralysis by analysis, 61–62
Pay for results, 84
Payment plans, 82
Persistent marketing, 44
Personal visit, 86
Persuasion principle, 204–205
Pizza industry, 18–21. *See also*
    Domino's Pizza
Points of Contact, 58–59
Positioning, 95–96
Price and return on investment
    (ROI), 38
Price:
    comparison, 109–110
    perceived value, 90
Pricing tricks, 89–93
Primacy, 95–96
Proactive, being, 178–180
Proof to bolster credibility, 48–49

Qualifications for expertise, 50
Quick evaluations by consumers, 2
Quid pro quo, 6–7, 36, 194

RackSpace Managed Hosting,
    117–118
Reality in Advertising (Reeves), 31
Rebates, 92–93
Recency, 96

Recognition, 50
Recommendations, 97
Reeves, Rosser, 31–32, 93
Referrals, 71
RE/MAX real estate, 122–123
Replication speed, 134–135, 141–142
Response mechanism in ads, 59
Return on investment (ROI), *see* High ROI offer
Risk reversal:
    free support, 84–85
    loss leaders, 82–83
    money-back guarantee, 80–82
    overview of, 80–81
    pay for results, 84
    payment plans, 82
    tactics, 81–86
    try before buying, 85
    warranties, 83

Salesmen, note to, 207–210
Sales process, 9–10, 53, 89, 162–163
Scam, definition of, 7
Scarcity, 86–87
Science of marketing, 99–100
Search Engine Tactics (Joyner), 145
Second Glass, selling:
    additions, 70–71
    consulting, service, and, 69
    continuity products, 67–68
    cross-sell, 65–66
    delivery techniques for, 64–65
    education and, 69
    follow-up, 66–67
    insurance, warranties, and, 70
    overview of, 60, 63–64
    package deals, 69–70
    recipes for, 68–69
    referrals, 71
    upsell, 65
Self, selling:
    believability and, 200–201
    Big Four Questions and, 189–192, 196–197
    Great Formula and, 202–203
    high ROI offer and, 200

    overview of, 183–184
    salesman and, 207
    in three seconds, 189
    Touchstone, 197–200
    Word of Mouth and, 203, 206
Service due reminders, 73
Shady persuasion, 193–195
Sheen, Martin, 49
Sheldrake, Rupert, 100
Sign Up step, 149, 152–153
Simplicity of Touchstone, 41–42
Sit N' Sleep, 119–120
Social proof, 48
Software products, 84–85
Sounds, 131
Special events, 74–75
Special offer, 26, 27–28
StartBlaze, 144–145, 156
Starting point, Irresistible Offer as, 23
Success, key to, 180
Sugarman, Joe, 79
Support, free, 84–85
Surprise, tactic of, 185–187

Target Behavior, 153–154
Technical proof, 48
Testimonials, 48
Testing, 61–62, 70
Thank you cards, 72
Think and Grow Rich (Hill), 178–180
Thirsty Crowd, presenting offer to, 56–57, 60
Thirty minutes or free guarantee, 86
Tongue-tied, being, during three seconds, 13
Touchstone:
    of Army, 114–115
    of Caterpillar Tractor, 121
    of Circuit City, 120–121
    of Columbia House Records, 43–45
    description of, 39–42
    of Domino's Pizza, 23, 43, 171–172
    of Federal Express, 45–46

of Fox News, 116–117
of Lexus, 176–177
of Maytag, 121
of Merle Norman Cosmetics, 123–124
of Mrs. Fields Cookies, 124
of Nordstrom's, 122
of RackSpace Managed Hosting, 117–118
of RE/MAX real estate, 122–123
for salesman, 208–209
for selling self, 197–200
of Sit N' Sleep, 119–120
stylistic elements of, 41–42
as ultimate virus, 169–172
of *Wall Street Journal*, 116
of WINS Radio, 115–116
Traffic exchange system, 144–145
Training step, 155–159
Transmission:
  for affiliate marketing systems, 159–160
  of information, 46
Tricking customers, 39
Triple money back, 86
Trust, 46, 139
Try before buying, 85
Turning down deals, 194–195

Uniqueness, 93–94
Unique Selling Proposition (USP), 27, 29–33
Unspoken Inner Dialogue, 9–10, 54
Upsell, 65
Urgency, 78–79, 108

Value:
  added, 79–80
  perceived, and price increase, 90–91
Video Professor computer learning CDs, 63
Viral marketing, 127–128

Viral Systems, *see* Word of Mouth marketing
Virulence:
  of biological virus, 133–135
  Copulation Rate and, 135–138
  measurement of, 143–146
  of Word of Mouth virus, 139–143
Virus:
  biological, 128–129
  Copulation Rate and, 135–138
  language as, 130
  Touchstone as ultimate, 169–172
  virulence of, 133–135, 139–143
Vitale, Joe, 88

Wall Street Journal, 116
Wal-Mart, 30–31
Warranties, selling, 70, 83
What's in it for me?, 12–13
WINS Radio, 115–116
Word of Mouth marketing:
  believability and, 169
  biological virus and, 128–129
  decreasing steps in sales process and, 162–163
  delivery mechanisms, 130–133, 172–175, 177–180
  ease and, 161–162
  Entry Point, 151–152
  excellence and, 163
  frame and, 150–151, 204–205
  general model of, 146–150
  high ROI and, 38–39, 97, 168
  incentives and, 164–166
  Irresistible Offer and, 166–167
  language as virus, 128, 130
  mechanisms of, 127–128
  overview of, 125–127
  selling self and, 203, 206
  Sign Up step and, 149, 152–153
  Target Behavior, 153–154
  Training step, 155–159
  transmission, 159–160
Words, 132, 166

How to Claim Your FREE $397 in Software and Audio Recordings

Plus a few extra secrets that will show you how to dramatically increase your profits today (not next year).

As a special thank-you gift for purchasing *The Irresistible Offer*, we have included an exclusive package of software and audio recordings which retail for $397.

Sadly, most people read books and then the knowledge they have acquired does much like the copy of the book they read: it collects dust.

These gifts were specially designed to help you get the most out of your experience with this book. Based on proven learning psychology tactics, the free software and audio recordings will not only ensure you more completely learn what you have read in *The Irresistible Offer*, but also stimulate you into action.

Also included are special activities and exercises to help you gain an immediate increase in profit in your business today.

You'll learn about that and more when you follow these steps to claim your $397 gift:

Step 1. **Go to this URL:**
   http://www.TheIrresistibleOffer.com/purchased

Step 2. **Authenticate**
   You will be prompted to open the book to a certain page and then find a particular word. This is our way of verifying that you purchased the book.

Step 3. **Enjoy**
   You'll find some extra surprises in there we didn't tell you about as well.

   See you there!

Mark Joyner

Author, *The Irresistible Offer*

P.S. Did you know that there is one thing you can do today that could increase your sales by 50% without any additional effort on your part? Follow the 3 steps above to find out what it is. You'll be pleasantly surprised by how easy this is.

9 780471 738947